Bible Study for
Young Adults

O9-BHL-737

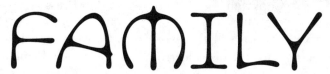

FAMILY
Finding Who We Are
and How We Belong

James Hawkins

Abingdon Press
Nashville

Family: Finding Who We Are and How We Belong
20/30: Bible Study for Young Adults

by James Hawkins

ISBN 0-687-02716-0

This book is printed on acid-free paper.

MANUFACTURED IN THE UNITED STATES OF AMERICA

04 05 06 07 08 09 10 11 12 13—10 9 8 7 6 5 4 3 2 1

CONTENTS

MEET THE WRITER

JIM HAWKINS is a United Methodist pastor, currently serving in Smyrna, Delaware. A graduate of Northwestern University, Jim's first career was in journalism. After a short and exciting stint as a reporter for a daily newspaper in Southern California, he responded to God's calling him to pastoral ministry, a different kind of news business. He graduated from Wesley Theological Seminary and has served as a pastor in the Peninsula-Delaware Conference. In addition to his pastoral duties, Jim writes for *FaithLink*.

Jim is married to Kathleen, who is the executive director of The United Methodist Foundation in the Eastern Pennsylvania and Peninsula-Delaware conferences. In his free time, Jim loves music (particularly singing), cooking, eating Kathleen's much better cooking, and traveling.

WELCOME TO 20/30: BIBLE STUDY FOR YOUNG ADULTS

The *20/30* Bible study series is offered for postmodern adults who want to help structure their own discoveries—in life, in relationships, in faith. In each of the volumes of this series, you will have the opportunity to use your personal experiences in life and faith to examine the biblical texts in new ways. Each session offers biblical themes and images that have the power to shape contemporary human life.

The Power of Images

An image has evocative power. You can see, hear, smell, taste, and touch the image in your imagination. It also has the power to evoke memory and to inform ideas and feelings. Placing Christmas ornaments on a tree evokes memories of past Christmas celebrations or of circumstances surrounding the acquisition of the ornament. As an adult you may remember making the ornament as a gift for your mother, father, or another important person in your life. You may experience once again all the feelings you had when you gave this gift.

An image also informs and gives shape to themes and ideas such as hope, faith, love, and compassion. The image of the ornament gives a particular shape to love because each Christmas someone carefully places it on the tree. Love becomes specific and easy to identify.

Biblical Images

The Bible offers an array of powerful and evocative images through stories, parables, poems, proverbs, and sermons. Jesus used a variety of familiar images: a woman seeking a lost coin, a merchant finding a pearl, seeds and plants, and cups that are clean on the outside but dirty on the inside. Such images transcend time and place and speak to people today. A story about a Samaritan who helped a wounded person says far more than the simple assertion that loving a neighbor means *being* a neighbor. Each of the volumes in this series connects familiar, contemporary experiences with scriptural content through a shared knowledge of theme and image.

Experience, Faith, Growth, and Action

Each volume in this series is designed to help you explore ways in which your experience links with your faith, and how deepening your faith expands your life experiences. As a prompt for reflection, each volume has several real-life **Case Studies.** Additional activities in the **Service Learning Options** offer a number of ways to be involved in specific service or learning opportunities. Activities in each session suggest ways to engage you or a group with the themes and images in the Bible.

A core Christian belief affirms that God's graceful presence and activity moves through all creation. This series is designed to support your encounters with God in a community of faith through Scripture, reflection, and dialogue. One goal of such encounters is to enhance your individual and shared commitment to serve others in the hope that they too might experience God's graceful presence.

HOW TO USE THIS RESOURCE

Each session of this resource includes similar components or elements:
- a statement of the issue or question to be explored
- several "voices" of persons who are currently dealing with that issue
- exploration of biblical passages relative to the question raised
- "Bible 101" boxes that provide insight about the study of the Bible
- questions for reflection and discussion
- suggested individual and group activities designed to bring the session to life
- optional case studies (found in the back of the book)
- various service learning activities related to the session (found in the back of the book)

Choices, Choices, Choices

Collectively, these components mean one thing: *choice.* You have choices to make concerning how to use each session of this resource.

Want just the nitty-gritty Bible reading, reflection, and study for personal or group use? Then focus your attention on just those components during your study time.

Like starting with real-life stories about issues then moving into how the Bible might be relevant? Start with the "voices" and move on from there. Use the "voices" to encourage group members to speak about their own experiences.

Prefer highly charged discussion encounters where many different viewpoints can be heard? Start the session with the biblical passages, followed by the questions and group activities. Be sure to compare the ideas found in the "Bible 101" boxes with your current ideas for more discussion.

Want the major challenge of applying biblical principles to a difficult problem? After reading the biblical material, read one of the case studies, using the guidelines provided on page 14; or get involved with one of the service learning options described in the back of the book.

Great Versatility

This resource has been designed for many different uses. Some persons will use this resource for personal study and reflection. Others will want to explore the work with a small group of friends. Still others will see this book as a different type of Sunday school resource.

Spend time thinking about your own questions, study habits, and learning styles and those of your small group. Then use the guidelines mentioned above to fashion each session into a unique Bible study session to meet those requirements.

Highly Participatory

As you will see, the Scriptures, "voices," commentary, and experiences of group members will provide an opportunity for an active, engaging time together. The greatest challenge for a group leader might be "crowd control"—being sure everyone has the chance to put his or her ideas into the mix!

The Scriptures will help you and those who study with you to make connections between real-life issues and the Bible. This resource values and encourages personal participation as a means to understand and appreciate the intersection of personal belief with God's ongoing work in each and every life.

ORGANIZING A GROUP

Learning with a small group of persons offers certain advantages over studying by yourself. First, you will probably encounter different opinions and ideas, making the experience of Bible study a richer and more challenging event. Second, any leadership responsibilities can be shared among group members. Third, different persons will bring different talents. Some will be deep thinkers while other group members will be creative giants. Some persons will be newcomers to the Bible; their questions and comments will help others clarify their deeply held assumptions.

So how does one go about forming a small group? Follow the steps below and see how easy this task can be.

- **Read through the resource carefully.** Think about the ideas presented, the questions raised, and the exercises suggested. If the sessions of this work excite you, it will be easier for you to spread your enthusiasm to others.

- **Spend some time thinking about church members, friends, and coworkers who might find the sessions of this resource interesting.** On a sheet of paper, list two characteristics or talents you see in each person that would make him or her an attractive Bible study group member. Some talents might include "deep thinker," "creative wizard," or "committed Christian." Remember: The best small group has members who differ in learning styles, talents, ideas, and convictions but who respect the dignity and integrity of the other members.

- **Make a list of potential group members that doubles your target number.** For instance, if you would like a small group of seven to ten members, be prepared to invite fourteen to twenty persons.

- **Once your list of potential candidates is complete, decide on a tentative location and time.** Of course, the details can be negotiated with those persons who accept the invitation; but you need to sound definitive and clear to perspective group members. "We will initially set Wednesday night from 7 to 9 P.M. at my house for our meeting time" will sound more attractive than "Well, I don't know either when or where we would be meeting; but I hope you will consider joining us."

- **Make initial contact with prospective group members short, sweet, and to the point.** Say something like, "We are putting together a Bible study using a different kind of resource. When would be a good time to show you the resource and talk about the study?" Establishing a special time to make the invitation takes the pressure off the prospective group member to make a quick decision.

- **Show up at the decided time and place.** Talk with each prospective member individually. Bring a copy of the resource with you. Show each person what excites you about the study and mention the two unique characteristics or talents you feel he or she would offer the group. Tell each person the initial meeting time and location and how many weeks the small group will meet. Also mention that the need for a new time or location could be discussed during the first group meeting. Ask for a commitment to come to the first session. Thank individuals for their time.

- **Give a quick phone call or e-mail to thank all persons for their consideration and interest.** Remind persons of the time and location of the first meeting.

- **Be organized.** Use the first group meeting to get acquainted. Briefly describe the seven sessions. Have a book for each group member, and discuss sharing responsibilities for leadership.

PREPARING TO LEAD

So the responsibility to lead the group has fallen upon you? Don't sweat it. Follow these simple suggestions and not only will you prepare to lead, you will also find that your mind and heart are open to encounter the Christ who is with you.

- **Pray.** Find a quiet place where you will not be interrupted. Have your Bible, the *20/30* book, paper, and pen handy. Ask for God's guidance and inspiration as you prepare for the session.

- **Read.** Look up all the Bible passages. Take careful notes about the ideas, statements, questions, and activities in the session. Record ideas and insights that occur to you as you read.

- **Think about group members.** Which ones like to think about ideas, concepts, or problems? Which ones need to "feel into" an idea by storytelling, worship, prayer, or group activities? Which ones are the "actors" who prefer a hands-on or participatory approach? Which ones might help you lead the session? Pray for each of the persons.

- **Think about the learning area and supplies.** What might you do with the place where you meet in order to enhance the experiences and activities of the session? Make a list of things, such as poster paper, pens or pencils, paper, markers, large white paper, supplies for more creative activities, Bibles, music, hymnals, or any other supplies you might need for the activities in the session.

- **Think about special arrangements.** You may need to make special arrangements: inviting a guest speaker, planning an activity that occurs outside the regular time and place, or acquiring audiovisual equipment, for example.

- **Pray.** After you have thought through all the steps listed above, thank God for any insights or inspirations you have had.

Using the Activity Icons

20/30 volumes include activity boxes marked with icons or images that indicate the kind of activity described in the box. The icons are intended to help you make decisions about which activities will best meet the needs of your group.

Start. A get-acquainted and worship activity that introduces the focus of the session.

 Discuss. Activities designed to stimulate large-group discussion.

 Small Group. Activities designed to stimulate discussion and reflection in groups of two or three persons. See the section "Using Break-out Groups" on pages 15-16.

 Bible. A Bible study activity that lists specific Scriptures. Participants will use the Bible.

 Look Closer. An activity designed to promote deeper, reflective awareness for an individual or for a group. The activity may call for use of resources such as Bible dictionaries or commentaries.

 Create. An activity designed for using a variety of creative art forms: drawing, sculpting, creating a mobile or a collage, or writing a poem or story.

 Case Study. An activity designed to explore and discuss a unique case study related to the session content or one of the case studies included in the back of the book.

 Serve. An activity that invites the group to discuss and engage in service to others. May relate directly to session content or to one of the service options in the back of the book.

 Music. An activity that uses music. May invite listening to a CD or singing a hymn, for example.

 Close. A closing activity that invites worship, celebration, or commitment to some specific action as a result of experiencing the session.

CHOOSING TEACHING OPTIONS

This young adult series was designed, written, and produced out of an understanding of the attributes, concerns, joys, and faith issues of young adults. With great care and integrity, this image-based print resource was developed to connect biblical events and relationships with contemporary, real-life situations of young adults. Its pages will promote Christian relationships and community, support new biblical learning, encourage spiritual development, and empower faithful decision-making and action.

This study is well suited to young adults and may be used confidently and effectively; but with the great diversity within the young adult population, not every line of this study will be written "just for you." To be most relevant, some portions of the study material need to be tailored to fit your particular group. Adjustments for a good fit involve making choices from options offered by the resource. This customizing may be done easily by a designated leader who is familiar with the layout of the resource and the young adults who are using it.

What to Expect

In this study, Scripture and real-life images mesh together to provoke a personal response. Young adults will find themselves thinking, feeling, imagining, questioning, making decisions, professing faith, building connections, inviting discipleship, taking action, and making a difference. Scripture is at the core of each session. Scenarios weave in the dimensions of real life. Narrative and text boxes frame plenty of teaching options to offer young adults.

Each session is part of a cohesive volume and also designed to stand alone. One session is not dependent on knowledge or experience accumulated from other sessions. A group leader can freely choose from the teaching options in an individual session without wondering about how it might affect the other sessions.

A Good Fit

For a better fit, alter the session based on what is known about the young adult participants. Young adults are a diverse constituency with varied experiences, interests, needs, and values. There is really no single defining characteristic that links young adults. Specific information about the age, employment status, household, personal relationships, and lifestyle among participants will equip a leader to make choices that ensure a good fit.

■ **Customize.** Read through the session. Notice how scenarios and teaching options move from integrating Scripture and real-life dimensions to inviting a response.

■ **Look at the case studies.** How real is the presentation of real life? Say that the main character is a professional, white male, married, in his early twenties, and caught in a workplace dilemma that entangles his immediate superior and a subordinate from his division. Perhaps your group members are mostly college students and recent graduates, unmarried, and still on the way to being "settled." There are many differences between the man in the scenario and these group members.

As a leader, you could choose to eliminate the case study, substitute it with another scenario from the case studies in the back of the book, claim the validity of the dilemma and shift the spotlight from the main character to the subordinate, or modify the description of the main character. Break-out groups based on age or employment experience might also be used to accommodate the differences and offer a better fit.

■ **Look at the teaching options.** How are the activities propelling participants toward a personal response? Perhaps the Scripture study requires more meditative quiet than is possible and a more academic, verbal, or artistic approach would offer a better fit. Maybe more direct decisions or actions would fit better than more passive or logical means. Try to keep a balance, though, that allows participants to "get out of their head" to reflect and also to move toward action.

Conceivably, there could just be too much in any one session. As a leader, you can pick and choose among teaching options, substitute case studies, take two meetings to do one session, and adapt any process to make a better fit. The tailoring process can be evaluated as adjustments are made. Judge the fit every time you meet. Ask questions that gauge relevance, and assess how the resource has stretched minds, encouraged discipleship, and changed lives.

USING BREAK-OUT GROUPS

20/30 break-out groups are small groups that encourage the personal sharing of lives and the gospel. The word *break-out* is a sweeping term that includes a variety of small group settings. A break-out group may resemble a Bible study group, an interest group, a sharing group, or other types of Christian fellowship groups.

Break-out groups offer young adults a chance to belong and personally relate to one another. Members are known, nurtured, and heard by others. Young adults may agree and disagree while maximizing the exchange of ideas, information, or options. They might explore, confront, and resolve personal issues and feelings with empathy and support. Participants can challenge and hold one another accountable to a personalized faith and stretch its links to real life and service.

Forming Break-out Groups

As you look through this book, you will see an icon that says "Small Group," which indicates that the total group of participants will be divided for a particular activity. Break-out groups will differ from one session to the next. Variations may involve the size of the group, how the group is divided, or the task of the group. Break-out groups may also be used to accommodate differences and help tailor the session plan for a better fit. In some sessions, specific group assembly instructions will be provided. For other sessions, decisions regarding the size or division of small groups will be made by the designated leader. Break-out groups may be in the form of pairs or trios, family-sized groups of three to six members, or groups of up to ten members.

They may be arranged simply by grouping persons seated next to one another or in more intentional ways by common interests, characteristics, or life experience. Consider creating break-out groups according to age; gender; type of household, living arrangements, or love relationships; vocation, occupation, career, or employment status; common or built-in connections; lifestyle; values or perspective; or personal interests or traits.

Membership

The membership of break-out groups will vary from session to session, or even within specific sessions. Young adults need to work at knowing and being known, so that there can be a balance between break-out groups that are more similar and those that reflect greater diversity. There may be times when more honest communication, trust, or accountability may be desired; and group leaders will need to be free to self-select members for small groups.

It is important for *20/30* break-out groups to practice acceptance and to value the worth of others. The potential for small groups to encourage personal sharing and significant relationships is enhanced when members agree to exercise active listening skills, keep confidences, expect authenticity, foster trust, and develop ways of loving one another. All group members contribute to the development and function of break-out groups. Designated leaders especially need to model manners of hospitality and help ensure that each group member is respected.

Invitational Listening

Consider establishing an "invitational listening" routine that validates the perspective and affirms the voice of each group member. After a question or statement is posed, pause and allow time to think—not all persons think on their feet or talk out loud to think. Then, initiate conversation by inviting one group member, by name, to talk. This person may either choose to talk or to "pass." Either way, this person is honored and is offered an opportunity to speak and be heard. This person carries on the ritual by inviting another group member, by name, to speak. The process continues until all have been invited, by name, to talk. As each one invites another, the responsibility of acceptance and hospitality in the break-out groups is shared among all its members.

Study group members break out to belong, to share the gospel, to care, and to watch over one another in Christian love. "So deeply do we care for you that we are determined to share with you not only the gospel of God but also our own selves, because you have become very dear to us" (1 Thessalonians 2:8).

FAMILY: FINDING WHO WE ARE AND HOW WE BELONG

None of us sprang to life on our own. Each one of us is part of a family. We are sons or daughters. Some of us are sisters or brothers, fathers or mothers, aunts or uncles, and cousins of all varieties (including second cousins once removed). We did not raise ourselves. We are part of a family, even if we live alone, and even if we are alienated from the members of our family.

But what, exactly, is a family? Is it a married couple with 2.3 children, a dog, and a minivan? couples without children? single adults? groups of friends? church groups? colleagues at work? The notion of "family" encompasses all these forms and more. In our study, it includes a quality of relationship shaped and nurtured by relationship with God, a relationship that encourages mutual growth in love of God, self, and neighbor through our interactions with those we identify as "family."

This resource will help us explore our questions about family with insights, images, and stories from Scripture. Each session delves into specific issues about family and contains suggestions about how an individual or group can use the session to look at family from a Christian perspective.

Five Friends

In this volume we will listen in on five friends.

- Bill—Bill is married to Chandra, and they have a young son, Bill Jr. Bill's parents are still married to each other. Bill wonders if he can raise a family with the negative societal pressures surrounding them.
- Jan—Jan's father died when she was thirteen, her brother was ten, and her sister was eight. Jan is convinced that when her mother died a year ago it was because she was consumed with grief and with working to take care of Jan and her siblings. Jan is single.
- Maria—Maria's parents are still married to each other. Maria is single and just broke up with her boyfriend a couple months ago. She wonders whether she will ever get married and have a "family of her own."
- Ryan—Ryan was twelve when his parents divorced. His mother remarried, but Ryan does not like his stepfather or his two stepsiblings. Since Ryan moved out of the house, he rarely sees his family. Ryan is single.
- Trevor—Trevor's parents divorced when he was 3. His mother has been married three times, and his father has been married twice and is now living with his girlfriend. His father is an alcoholic, and his mother tends

to marry men she hopes to "save." Trevor lives with his girlfriend, Sandy, and has no intention of getting married.

We may have some things in common with some of these friends. Some of them may be very different than we are. However, as we overhear their discussions, we may discover that they ask some of the same questions many of us ask.

An Overview of the Sessions

In Session 1, we will look at the value of family. Why should we care about family if we can make it on our own? What is the value of family for single persons? How does our Christian faith inform the value of family in all its configurations?

Session 2 provides an opportunity to define what we mean when we say the word *family*. What models exist for a family? What is the biblical model for a family, or is there more than one kind of family in the Bible? How does Christian faith help us to define *family*?

During Session 3, we will explore the issue of family and personal identity. What does family contribute to a person's identity? What is the role of nature versus the role of nurture? Or do we create our own identities?

In Session 4, we look at brokenness in the family. The term *dysfunctional family* has almost become a cliché in our society. Yet, what is the difference between a relatively functional, healthy family and a dysfunctional, broken one?

Session 5 explores the characteristics of healthy families. What makes healthy families healthy? Does a family have to be perfect in order to be healthy?

During Session 6, we will continue looking at healthy families and in particular what we can do to create healthy families. How do single adults and couples without children build and nurture family life? What can communities and institutions do to contribute to family life?

Finally, in Session 7, we will explore the idea of the church as God's family. What does it mean to look to "family" as an image of contemporary Christian life? How does Scripture use the metaphor of family to describe the church?

The Challenge

This resource challenges many of our presuppositions about family. We may be surprised to discover some of the nuances of the biblical witness. We may reconsider some aspects of family life that we have not held in high regard. We may find new ways to enrich our own family life, whether we are single or married, raising children or without children. May this resource be a blessing for you as you explore ways as to how an experience of family can enrich your daily life.

Family: Finding Who We Are and How We Belong

THE VALUE OF FAMILY

This session explores the value of family and why we should care about family when we can make it on our own.

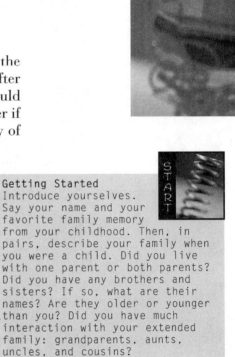

CASE STUDY

Maria: When I look at my parents, I see the ideal. They are still happily married after thirty-one years and three children. I would love to have what they have, but I wonder if I will ever get married and have a family of my own.

Ryan: Your childhood sounds like a 1950s sitcom. Mine was more like a horror movie. I'll never forget the day I came home from school and found my Dad with another woman. As it turned out, it wasn't his first affair. Mom couldn't take it any more, and she forced him to move out. But my stepfather isn't much better. He might be faithful to Mom, but he's a jerk; and his kids are spoiled brats. I've been much happier since I moved out of the house. I rarely see my family any more. Why should I care about family when I can make it on my own? I think family is overrated.

Getting Started
Introduce yourselves. Say your name and your favorite family memory from your childhood. Then, in pairs, describe your family when you were a child. Did you live with one parent or both parents? Did you have any brothers and sisters? If so, what are their names? Are they older or younger than you? Did you have much interaction with your extended family: grandparents, aunts, uncles, and cousins?

START

Overrated?
Review the discussion with the five friends. Of the five, whose opinions resonate the most with you? Why? With whose opinions do you most strongly disagree? Why? Poll your group. Does your group agree most with Bill, Jan, Maria, Ryan, or Trevor? Why?

Advice Columnist
You have been hired to write an advice column, "Ask Pat," for your local newspaper. Imagine that one of the five friends writes you a letter that reflects the views stated in the discussion. Write an advice column in response to that letter. Tell the group which friend you chose, and read your advice column.

Looking Back in Time
Think about when you were a child. Imagine that your art teacher asked you to draw a picture of your family. Include not only your family members, but also any pets. After you have completed your picture, find a partner. Look at your drawings. Discuss your answers to these questions: When you were a child, what would you have said was the most important part of your home life? As you look back, what would you now say was the most important part of your home life? If there is a difference in your answers, why has that changed?

Trevor: I couldn't agree with you more. That's why Sandy and I are living together. I think it's great. We have all the benefits of family without the hassles. Mom says that we're living in sin, but she hasn't exactly been a poster child for family values. She's been married three times, and her current husband is as much of a loser as her first two.

Jan: I can understand why Ryan and Trevor are gun-shy about commitment. My parents had a great marriage, but Dad died fifteen years ago; and Mom never got over it. She was dedicated to the three of us kids, but she had no life other than us. She died last year after my little sister graduated from college. She was so focused on family that she never lived.

Bill: I disagree with Ryan and Trevor. Family isn't overrated. If anything, it's underrated. I'm the only one of us who is married and the only one with a child, so obviously I believe family is important. But when I think about being good parents, I don't know if we can do it on our own. There are so many negative societal pressures; and when I think about the lack of good, strong, responsible male role models, I wonder if I am a good father or not. I wonder what kind of father my son will be.

CHANGING FAMILY

Ryan told Maria that her childhood sounds like a 1950s sitcom. Families like Maria's family of origin are, in fact, less common today than forty years ago. In 1960, married couples with children made up 44 percent of all households in the United States. In 2000, that percentage dipped to just 24 percent of all households. Meanwhile, the number of households of persons living alone, particularly women living alone, has increased dramatically. The makeup of households with children is also changing. In 1970, 89 percent of households with children were two-parent families. By 2000, that figure had dropped: Seventy percent of households with children were two-parent families; 22 percent were headed by a single mother; and five percent were headed by a single father.[1] John Leo questioned the perception that nuclear families are dwindling and pointed out that 62 percent of our children are still living in them.[2]

Family has been valued for many reasons over the years: to enhance physical survival, to produce and raise children, and to bring stability to society, to name a few. With more and more Americans living alone, is family obsolete? Ryan voiced a common sentiment: Why should I care about family when I can make it on my own? For those who seek to live as faithful Christians, how does faith help us value family? Of what value is faith as we seek ways to value family bonds? How does valuing the family help us discover who we are and how we belong in this world? As we expand our definitions of family and begin to look at the dynamic of human relationship as defined by Christian faith, we begin to see the potential for claiming the value of family.

One reason for the increase in the number of households of single women is that many wait longer to marry than was common forty years ago.[3] My wife's grandmother was one of four daughters and the only one to have children. Family legend holds that Great Aunt Louise married only because, at the time, society frowned on a single woman owning property in her own name.

Since she wanted to own a house, she married. The other great aunts, Florence and Elsie, never married. In their younger years it was unusual for a woman to live alone, so they lived together until they died in their nineties. Today, single women, like single men, can own property. Single women, as well as single men, can have productive, lucrative careers. So if the purpose of family is to enhance physical survival, particularly for women, family is no longer a necessity. Physically, most of us can make it on our own.

If the value of family is simply to produce and raise children, does that mean that those families who do not have children are not legitimate families? Hannah felt so. She lived thousands of years ago when it was not uncommon for a man to have more than one wife. Hannah did not have any children with her husband Elkanah; but Elkanah did have children with his other wife, Peninnah. Peninnah belittled Hannah for being childless. Hannah was so tormented that she prayed, "O LORD of hosts, if only you will look on the misery of your servant, and remember me, and not forget your servant, but will give to your servant a male child, then I will set him before you" (1 Samuel 1:11). Hannah did have a child, Samuel, who grew to become a prophet. But are only those families with children "real" families? Have those who remain childless not prayed fervently enough? How do childless couples understand themselves, and how do they create meaning in their relationship?

The Bible offers other models of the marriage relationship. In the New Testament, the married couple Priscilla and Aquila are mentioned frequently by Paul (Acts 18:1-19; Romans 16:3; 1 Corinthians 16:19; 2 Timothy 4:19). No evidence exists that

Family: Finding Who We Are and How We Belong

Priscilla and Aquila had children, yet they are clearly models of faithfulness. The biblical witness extends beyond the need to have and raise children. Other values are at work.

Changing Family
Review the section "Changing Family." As a group, discuss your responses to these questions: What evidence do you see that in the US the family has changed? What evidence do you see that it is continuing to change? On a large piece of paper or on a chalkboard, create two columns—one entitled "Positive," the other "Negative." Brainstorm ways in which these changes are positive and ways in which they are negative, and list them in the appropriate column. When complete, look at the responses. As a group, did you list more positive or negative changes?

GOOD NOT TO BE ALONE

According to Genesis, the first family was created for an important reason: "Then the LORD God said, 'It is not good that the man should be alone; I will make him a helper as his partner'" (2:18). So God created the birds and other animals, but none of these living creatures was an adequate partner for the man. It was only when God created another human being, a woman, that the man was no longer alone. Genesis reminds us that we are not created to live totally alone. We are created to live in community, to live connected with other human beings. We need to be connected with other people in order to thrive.

Good Not to Be Alone
In Genesis 2:18, God said, "It is not good that the man should be alone." Form groups of three or four. Why do you think this is included in the Bible? Give examples that illustrate the truth that it is not good for a person to be alone.

FAMILY FOR SINGLE PEOPLE

What about single people? Does family have value for those who are not married? And if so, what form does family take?

Before I married at age 32, people would comment that because I did not have a family, I had more time to devote to work. I usually replied that while I was

Honoring Parents
Read the Bible 101 on page 24. If your parents do not depend on you in order to live, what can you do to keep this commandment to honor your father and mother? In what ways do our parents depend on us in today's culture? In your opinion, what values reside in continuing involvement with aging parents? with other aging people in extended families? List your ideas, first privately, then as a larger group.

Soundtrack
Think about your family when you were a child. What song could have been your family's theme song? Why? Before the group meets again, try to get a recording of that song. At the next gathering, have the members of the group come a little early to listen to the theme songs.

not married, I certainly was a family man. I was connected with my parents, sister, brother-in-law, nephew, and niece. I was connected with a family of close friends. I was connected with the family of the church. These relationships empowered me to thrive.

Perhaps you have a close network of friends who feel like family. Maybe you are part of a small group at your church that is nurturing. Or you may have shared a house or apartment with roommates who interacted much like a family. You may have discovered that your Christian faith infuses these relationships with a sense of family.

Bible 101
One of the most frequently cited of the Ten Commandments is "honor your father and your mother, so that your days may be long in the land that the LORD your God is giving you" (Exodus 20:12). Often, this passage is quoted to young children in order to coax them to listen to their parents. Yet the commandments were primarily aimed at adults who were full members of the covenant community. In this context, this commandment to honor your father and your mother shifts emphasis. Instead of being geared to young children to encourage them to behave, the commandment addresses adult children to care for their elderly parents. This was a particularly important value in the ancient Near East, long before social security, Medicare, and other safeguards for older persons. This remains an important value in our society, which often celebrates youth and views older adults as unproductive and burdens to their children.[4]

UNDERRATED?

In the opening section, Bill argued that family is not overrated. In his mind, it is underrated. Family values have been a topic of great discussion in the public arena in the last few years, with some advocating the 1950s sitcom norm and others dismissing such a traditional family structure as outdated at best and destructive at worst. The authors of the second edition of *From Culture Wars to Common Ground: Religion and the American Family Debate* argue that, by and large, two-parent families are better for children than single-parent families. While the authors do not call for a return to patriarchy, they do recommend that the ideal family "is the voluntary lifetime union of a woman and a man who parent their own children in a relationship characterized by love, justice and equal regard. In this relationship, both the woman and the man play important public (including paid employment) and private (domestic) roles. This union is neither a revocable contract between independent and equal parties nor mandated by an unchanging divine law which legitimates the subordination of women."[5] The authors highlight four trends that have weakened the family: "heightened individualism; the increased role of market forces and government bureaucracies in family life; . . . the powerful psychological shifts caused by these forces; and the lingering influence of patriarchy."[6]

The Christian faith can help us as we seek to strengthen the value of the family bond in all its forms. When we remember that God created us to live in relationship with others, when we learn how to love others by discovering how God loves us, when we care for others as brothers and sisters in Christ, when we stay connected to others through prayer, we celebrate the value of family in all configurations.

SMALL GROUP

Form groups of two or three. Imagine that you work for a dictionary publisher. You were hired to define words. Your new assignment is to define the word *family*. Take a few minutes to write out your definition. When you are done, discuss your definitions with your group. Bring your definitions with you for Session 2.

CLOSE

Close
Invite each group member to say one positive value of family while one person writes the responses on a large piece of paper or the board. Close with prayer, being sure to give thanks to God for the gift of family and all the positive values generated by the group.

[1] Reported in *Newscope*, March 30, 2001; page 3.
[2] Reported in *U.S. News & World Report*, May 28, 2001; page 12.
[3] *U.S. News & World Report*.
[4] From *Exodus*, by Terence E. Fretheim (John Knox Press, 1991); pages 231-2.
[5] From a review by Garrett Paul of *From Culture Wars to Common Ground: Religion and the American Family Debate* in *The Christian Century*, May 9, 2001.
[6] *The Christian Century*.

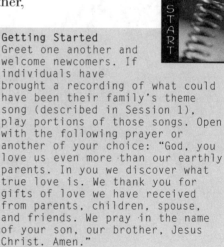

DEFINING FAMILY

This session explores a variety of definitions of family in the Bible and in contemporary culture.

WHAT IS A FAMILY?

Trevor: I don't understand all this talk about family values. It seems to come from narrow-minded folks who want the rest of us to fit into their definition of family. Sure, when I was a kid, I loved watching *The Cosby Show*. They all cared for each other, they laughed together a lot, and any problems they had were resolved in thirty minutes. I thought it would be great to have parents like Mr. and Mrs. Huxtable. I actually pretended that I was their second son; but that was just fiction, and that fiction was a lot better than my reality. Not only did Dad leave when I was three, but after the divorce, he wasn't around much. I would visit him every other weekend for the first couple years; but after that, I saw him only a few times a year. I found out a couple years ago that he stopped sending Mom child support checks when I was twelve. And my stepfathers? Let's just say

Getting Started
Greet one another and welcome newcomers. If individuals have brought a recording of what could have been their family's theme song (described in Session 1), play portions of those songs. Open with the following prayer or another of your choice: "God, you love us even more than our earthly parents. In you we discover what true love is. We thank you for gifts of love we have received from parents, children, spouse, and friends. We pray in the name of your son, our brother, Jesus Christ. Amen."

What Is a Family?
In what ways do you identify with any of the friends in their discussion? Which ones? How? When have you felt that other people—friends, relatives, society in general—judge your level of involvement with family? Explain.

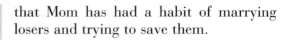

that Mom has had a habit of marrying losers and trying to save them.

Maria: Trevor, I'm sorry you haven't had the best family life. Ryan said before that my childhood sounds like a 1950s sitcom. Well, it wasn't. My parents weren't wealthy. Dad and Mom worked full-time, and even then they had to make some tough financial choices. My Dad loves fishing, and he really wanted his own fishing boat; but he made us a priority—saving for our education, buying our clothes. So he has waited, and he's going to buy himself a boat for his fifty-fifth birthday. Believe me, we had problems that weren't resolved in thirty minutes; but we kids always knew that Mom and Dad loved us and that somehow things were going to work out if we worked together as a family.

Ryan: If family is so important to you, why don't you get married and have some kids of your own?

Jan: Don't you think that's hitting below the belt? She just broke up with Juan a couple months ago, and they broke up because she wants to have children and he doesn't. You don't have to get married and have kids to be part of a family.

Ryan: Sorry I was so insensitive; but when I hear you talk about your family, I feel like you're judging me. It seems like you're looking down your nose at me because I don't think family is important. At times, I feel like a little kid again. I can't tell you how many times I overheard someone say, "Poor Ryan! You know, he comes from a broken home."

Bill: Ryan, there are times that I feel like you are judging both Maria and me because our families are still intact. Ever since Chandra and I got married, it seems like you won't have anything to do with me. You've written me off as an old married man, and it's only gotten worse since our baby was born.

Jan: You know who we sound like? We sound like my brother, sister, and me when we were kids. It seemed like we were fighting all the time, getting on one another's nerves, calling each other names. The five of us sound just like a family. To be honest, I've always looked at us as family, and that feeling has increased since Mom died last year.

Trevor: Maybe we need to think about how we understand family. Maybe family means more than being married and having kids.

Jan: That's what I think, Trevor.

> **TV Family**
> Families have been the center of television shows from the beginning. As you think of television families, which family most appeals to you? Why? Which family most repels you? Why? Talk about your answers with others in the group. Any common responses?

FITTING IN

In the friends' discussion, Trevor voiced his concern that talk about family values is an attempt of some people to make all of us fit into a narrow definition of family. Some view our society's definition of family as a married couple with 2.3 children, a dog, and a minivan.

While some families do fit that definition (though it is difficult to have .3 of a child), we know that is not the only form family can take. Many persons live in social groupings that function as families even though they might not meet the above criteria.

What about married couples who do not have children? What about single persons? What about single parents raising children?

> **Fitting In**
> Form small groups of three or four and talk about your answers to these questions: Which of the dictionary definitions of family comes closest to describing the most significant family relationship in your life? Does describing family as "a group of people united by certain convictions or a common affiliation" seem valid? Why or why not?

For the Joy
As a group, sing the hymn "For the Beauty of the Earth." Focus on the portion of the stanza that says: "For the joy of human love, / brother, sister, parent, child, / friends on earth and friends above, / for all gentle thoughts and mild; / Lord of all, to thee we raise / this our hymn of grateful praise." What types of families are addressed in this stanza? How can we "raise our hymn of grateful praise" to God for "the joy of human love?" In your group, discuss your responses. Which of these ideas are new to you? Which do you want to try?

Among the dictionary definitions of the word *family* are:

1. "a group of individuals living under one roof and usually under one head";
2. "a group of persons of common ancestry";
3. "a people or group of peoples deriving from a common stock";
4. "a group of people united by certain convictions or a common affiliation."[1]

These definitions point to a broader understanding of family.

Some examples of family using these broader definitions of family include:

- a group of friends who meet regularly to support and encourage one another;
- several young adults who share an apartment;
- a church-related small group that meets weekly for a shared meal, Bible study, prayer, and fellowship.

Each of these groups, and many others, can act as family units to provide nurture and care.

Bible 101
Scripture mentions several levels of family. The smallest family unit was what we today call the nuclear family, often called the "house." The house consisted of parents and their unmarried children and sometimes slaves or long-time guests who lived with the family. The father had most of the authority in the family (Deuteronomy 21:15-17; Ephesians 6:4; Colossians 3:18-21), although this was by no means absolute authority. The extended family, made up of two or more nuclear families with a common ancestor, was often called the "father's house." The extended family had special legal rights. For example, if one family was forced to sell property, members of the extended family had the right to keep the property within the family (Leviticus 25:25; Jeremiah 32:6-8). The largest family unit was the clan, made up of two or more extended families. A clan also descended from a common ancestor, though ties in addition to blood ties often united a clan. Members of a clan generally lived in the same area. The clan seems to have had few social functions. In the New Testament, the Christian community is often described as a new kind of family.[2]

SOME BIBLICAL FAMILY MODELS

The Bible contains a variety of family models. The Book of Exodus concentrates on Moses, who had an unusual family background. His family of origin was a nuclear family: His mother and father were married. Raising a child is never easy, but circumstances at the time in Egypt made parenting an even greater challenge for Hebrews. Pharaoh had ordered that all newborn boys be drowned in the Nile River. Moses' mother devised a plan to save her young son by placing him in a basket in the river. The baby was discovered by Pharaoh's daughter, who raised him as her son (Exodus 2:1-10).

Biblical Families
Read the accounts of Moses' family (Exodus 2:1-10), Ruth's family (Ruth 1:1-18), Esther's family (Esther 2:5-7), and Lydia's family (Acts 16:11-15). What surprises you about these four families? Do these families seem to fit your understanding of a biblical family? Why or why not? What connections do you make between these biblical images of family and those in contemporary culture? How can they help you as you think about the people in your life, both inside and outside the group you understand as your family?

The Book of Ruth focuses on an extended family: Elimelech, Naomi, their grown sons Mahlon and Chillion, and daughters-in-law Orpah and Ruth. The men in the family died, leaving Naomi, Orpah, and Ruth as widows. Orpah returned to her father's house, but Ruth refused to leave her mother-in-law. In an impassioned plea, Ruth said to Naomi, "Do not press me to leave you / or to turn back from following you! / Where you go, I will go; / where you lodge, I will lodge; / your people shall be my people, / and your God my God" (Ruth 1:16).

The Book of Esther centers on a Jewish family. Mordecai had raised his cousin Hadassah, also known as Esther, whose parents had died. After their deaths, Mordecai adopted Esther as his own daughter (Esther 2:7).

The Book of Acts records the conversion of Lydia, a wealthy businesswoman in Philippi. Lydia is depicted as the head of her household, although the exact nature of her household is not described. Lydia also became a leader in the church, and invited the infant Philippian church to meet in her home (Acts 16:11-15).

Acts also chronicles the life of Paul. Acts never indicates that Paul was married, and Paul states that he is not married (1 Corinthians 7:8); yet Paul was clearly connected with other people. He did not venture alone on his missionary journeys. Instead, he was always part of "a group of people united by certain convictions or a common affiliation." At first, his partner was Barnabas (Acts 13:1—15:39), followed later by Silas (15:40). Acts records that at various times Paul was joined by John Mark, Timothy, Priscilla and Aquila, and others.

CONTEMPORARY FAMILIES

Families in our society take many different forms. The 1950s sitcom model—with a breadwinning father, stay-at-home mother, and children—is not the only model for family households today. Of the approximately 100 million households in the United States in 1996, the largest segment is the two-earner married couple, with or without children, at 34 percent of all households. The second largest at 30 percent is single-person households, which includes those who have never married, those who are divorced, or those who are widowed. About 20 percent of households are married couples, with or without children, with only the man working outside the home. The remaining households are female-headed households with dependents (13 percent) and male-headed households with dependents (3 percent).[3]

CREATE

Write a poem or song lyric about family. This could be about your biological family, your close friends, or your church family. After a few minutes, read your work. Are the feelings you expressed happy? sad? hopeful? angry? ambivalent?

DISCUSS

Just Like a Family

Jan said that she has always looked on her friends as family. As a group, brainstorm your responses to this question: In what ways can a group of friends be just like a family? Then discuss your answers to the following question: In what ways is a group of friends not like a family?

Understanding family in a broader sense helps us value those familial relationships we may already enjoy—such as close friends, or church-related small groups—and can also encourage us to seek out new forms of family. God created us to live in community, for nurture, for caring, for support, for accountability. When we see other people, including our friends and fellow church members, as members of our family, we discover that we have a richer, more health-giving family life.

SERVE

Invite a social worker, perhaps one who works for a local school district, to come to your group's session. Ask your guest to come prepared to suggest ways members of your group can be helpful to families in need in your community. This could include one-time help, short-term help, and long-term help.

SMALL GROUP

Definitions
Form teams of two or three. Review your definition of *family* from Session 1. Answer the following questions with the members of your small group: After this session, how would you modify your definition? Why would you modify your definition?

CLOSE

Close
Join in singing "For the Beauty of the Earth." Ask group members to write the names of those persons who are family for them on small pieces of paper, with one name per piece of paper. Pass an offering plate or a basket around the group, and place the names in the offering plate or basket. Pray as a group, giving thanks to God for those who are family for you.

[1] From *Merriam-Webster's Collegiate Dictionary*, Tenth Edition (Merriam-Webster, Inc., 1993); pages 419-20.
[2] From *Harper's Bible Dictionary* (HarperCollins, 1973); pages 302-3.
[3] From "Diverse Forms of Family Life Merit Recognition," by Rosemary Radford Ruether, in *National Catholic Reporter*, June 16, 2000.

FAMILY AND IDENTITY

This session will explore how family contributes to a person's identity.

WHO AM I?

Jan: I'm worried about my sister getting married. She's only twenty-three. She's so young to make such a big commitment.

Maria: My mother was younger than that when she got married.

Jan: It's not just that she's twenty-three. I'm also worried that she's getting married for the wrong reason. Don't get me wrong; her fiancée, Greg, is a great guy. I wonder if the only reason Sara is getting married is because she wants to be part of a family. After Mom died, Sara's been at loose ends, feeling like little orphan Annie. I understand where she's coming from, because I feel like that, too, at times; but I think it would be a huge mistake to get married just so she can have a new identity as part of Greg's family.

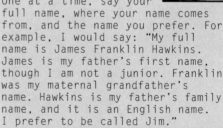

Getting Started

Greet one another and welcome any newcomers. One at a time, say your full name, where your name comes from, and the name you prefer. For example, I would say: "My full name is James Franklin Hawkins. James is my father's first name, though I am not a junior. Franklin was my maternal grandfather's name. Hawkins is my father's family name, and it is an English name. I prefer to be called Jim."

Lead the group in the following prayer, or pray extemporaneously: "O God, you created us in love. You created us in your image; male and female you created us. Thank you for our unique identity and for those people who helped shape who we are. Amen."

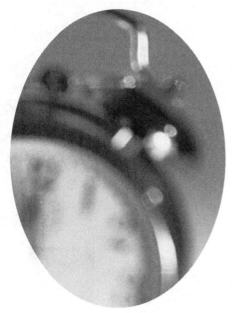

Ryan: I got saddled with a horrible identity because of my family. My parents separated when I was twelve, so from junior high on, I was always "Ryan, the problem kid from the broken home." It doesn't help any that my stepfather's a jerk, and everyone knew I hated him. While at times I used that label of "problem kid" as an opportunity to get away with all sorts of stuff, I always envied you, Bill. You've always been "Bill, the stable one," and you still are.

Bill: You envied me? That's the first I've heard that.

Ryan: It's true. You always seem so together.

Bill: My parents take most of the credit for that. They tried everything they could think of to help us grow up to be responsible adults. It wasn't always easy for them or for us. Believe me, I haven't always been so together. When I messed up, my parents made sure I knew they loved me. Yet they also made sure that I faced the consequences of my actions. Their theory was that that was the only way I would learn. Chandra and I hope to do the same thing with our son.

Trevor: I would like to give my parents most of the blame for the problems I've had in life, but I think that's a cop-out. Yes, my Dad would never get selected as Father of the Year. And, yes, my stepfathers haven't been much better. But I've made my own choices. If my life is going great, it's because I made the right choices. If my life is a mess, it's because I messed it up.

Maria: You don't think your family has shaped you at all?

Trevor: In some ways they have. I have my father's curly hair and my mother's dimples. Other than that, I'm a self-made man.

Maria: I can definitely see how my family has had a tremendous influence on making me who I am. I have a good job today, in part, because my parents sacrificed in order to send me to college. I try to treat people with respect because my parents taught me how, both by what they said and by what they did, to respect others and how to respect myself. Much of the reason I'm active in church today is because I was raised in church. And some day I want to have kids of my own so I can pass all that on to the next generation.

SHAPED BY FAMILY?

Trevor believes that while his physical attributes are a result of his family background—his hair is curly like his father's, and he has dimples much like his mother's—his identity was not influenced much by his family. Maria, Bill, and Ryan each see that who they are as adults was shaped by their families. Who is right? Are our identities set by our families? Are we self-made men and women who create our own identities?

Some people, like Bill and Maria, believe their family shaped their identity in positive ways. Bill credits his parents with helping him and his siblings grow into responsible adults by holding them accountable for their actions; he hopes to do the same for his son. Maria believes her parents positively influenced her by their sacrifices for her and their example. Other people, like Ryan, believe that their identity with their family is not always positive. As a teenager, Ryan felt identified as a problem child because of difficulties within his family.

All the friends' observations carry some degree of truth. Yes, it is true that our identities are shaped by our families; and it is also true that to some extent we are "self-made." Understanding how our identities are shaped can help us understand our feelings and our choices. Christians also take into account how their faith influences their identity within and outside families. As we become more conscious of these influences upon our identities, we may well begin to experience greater freedom in our daily decision making.

FAMILY IDENTITY IN THE BIBLE

Family played at least some role in shaping the identities of persons in the Bible. Individual lives are often placed in a family context, beginning with the very first book of the Bible, Genesis. Abram, for instance, the ancestor of the Hebrew people, is himself introduced as the son of Terah, who himself was a descendant of Shem, one of Noah's sons (Genesis 10:1; 11:10-29).

God called Abram to leave his family of origin and go to a new land. God promised, "I will make of you a great nation, and I will bless you, and make your name great, so that you will be a blessing. I will bless those who bless you, and the one who curses you I will curse; and in you all the families of the earth shall be blessed" (Genesis 12:2-3). The rest of Genesis follows the lives of Abram (who was later renamed Abraham) and his family: his wife Sarah; his sons Ishmael and Isaac; Isaac's

Take turns describing yourself in terms of your relationship with other people. For example, "I'm Mary and John's son," or "I am Wanda's sister," or "I am Sue's friend," or "I am Leroy's uncle." After each person has described themselves, discuss these questions: How do our relationships with other people help define who we are? Do our relationships define us in positive ways or in negative ways?

Many hymnals and songbooks contain hymns about family, such as "O Lord, May Church and Home Combine" and "The Family Prayer Song." Choose one to sing as a group. After you sing together, discuss your answers to these questions: What makes this hymn powerful? What could make it more powerful? In what ways, if any, does it address issues of identity in your family?

wife Rebekah and their sons Esau and Jacob; Jacob's wives Leah and Rachel and their many children. God's covenant with Abraham is passed down to Isaac, Jacob (who was later renamed Israel), and Israel's children.

The role of David's family is prominent in Scripture. The prophet Nathan voiced God's covenant with David: "Your house and your kingdom shall be made sure forever before me; your throne shall be established forever" (2 Samuel 7:16). Indeed David's descendants ruled as kings in Jerusalem until the Babylonian defeat of Judah hundreds of years later. Later, prophets like Isaiah looked for a coming messiah descended from David (Isaiah 9:2-7). Jesus is often referred to as the son of David. In fact, the Gospel of Matthew begins with a genealogy "of Jesus the Messiah, the son of David, the son of Abraham" (Matthew 1:1). The genealogy ties Jesus to a family that shaped his identity. The Gospel of Luke also includes a genealogy of Jesus, but Luke's genealogy stretches back to Adam (Luke 3:23-38).

Jesus' Family Tree
Read Matthew 1:1-16. Notice any surprises in Jesus' family tree? Look closer at some of the women included in the genealogy: Tamar (verse 3), Rahab (verse 5), Ruth (verse 5), and Bathsheba (listed as "the wife of Uriah" in verse 6). What do you know about these women? Use a Bible dictionary to find out more. Why does Matthew include these women in this genealogy? What does this tell us about Jesus' identity? Read Luke 3:23-38. Do you notice any other differences between Matthew and Luke? Why do you think Matthew's genealogy differs from Luke's? What does Luke's genealogy say to you about Jesus' identity?

Genealogy
Create a genealogy of your family. Go back as many generations as you can, and include as much description of each family member as you know. Is there anything that surprises you in your family? anything that makes you proud? anything that embarrasses you? Do you notice any patterns in your family? What does this genealogy tell us about your identity?

NATURE, NURTURE, OR OTHER?

If our families have at least some role in shaping our identities, is it because of nature or nurture? We are "a combination of genetic influences, parental and environmental influences, and peer pressure," writes Andrea DellaVecchio. "Just how much do genes influence the development of a child? Researchers have been seeking the answer to this question for many years. While there are no definitive answers, researchers have found that genetic factors

I.D. Please
Think about your own identity. Are you more a product of nature or nurture? Form small groups of three or four. Discuss your answer.

CREATE

Think about some of the characteristics of your family of origin. Create a family crest using crayons, markers, pencils, and poster board or paper. Display the family crest of each member of the group in your meeting space.

make an important contribution to the development of a child. But . . . researchers have also found that the environment plays a major role in that development. A warm and loving environment provides a secure place in which a child can develop abilities and talents which might otherwise have gone unrealized."[1]

While our families do play some role in shaping who we are, Trevor is right that often we blame our parents instead of taking personal responsibility for who we are. Several persons in the Bible clearly chose an identity for themselves. Moses, whose family background we explored in Session 2, had a choice. Would he identify with the Hebrews and the family who gave him birth, or would he choose the Egyptians and the family who raised him? Moses chose to identify himself with the Hebrew people when he saw an Egyptian beating a Hebrew slave, who was identified as "one of his kinsfolk" (Exodus 2:11-15).

Samuel, whose birth we looked at during Session 1, took his identity not from his birth family of Elkanah and Hannah, but from Eli, the priest who raised him (1 Samuel 1:20—3:21). Timothy, the son of a Jewish/Christian mother and a Greek/pagan father, chose to be a Christian. At the time, there was some controversy among the early Christians about whether one had to be a Jew before one could be a Christian. Since Timothy's mother was Jewish (meaning that Timothy would be considered Jewish) and his father was pagan (meaning that Timothy had not been circumcised), Paul decided that it would be best for Timothy to be circumcised (Acts 16:1-3).

When we discover how our identities have been shaped in families, we also discover more fully whom we are and why we behave the way we do. Our Christian faith can help us sort through the positive and negative influences of family, and help us—like Moses, Samuel, and Timothy before us—take personal responsibility for who we are and what we do. Our Christian faith also promises the possibility of transformation. We need not be trapped by the negative influences of nature and nurture; but we can be freed to be a new creation in Jesus Christ and discover a new identity as a child of God and a member of God's family, the church.

Bible 101

Jesus grew up within a family, and much of his identity came from his family. Luke records that early in his ministry, Jesus came to the synagogue in his hometown of Nazareth. Word of what he had done in other parts of Galilee preceded his homecoming, and his words in the synagogue were impressive. "All spoke well of him and were amazed at the gracious words that came from his mouth. They said, 'Is not this Joseph's son?'" (Luke 4:22). The reader can interpret that comment as positive ("My, Joseph's son certainly is a remarkable young man!"), or as negative ("Who does he think he is? We know he's just the son of Joseph the carpenter.").

Jesus' family identity was at times a source of conflict. At age 12, Jesus and his family traveled to Jerusalem for Passover. When Mary and Joseph left for home, they assumed Jesus was traveling with them in the group of travelers. They did not realize that Jesus stayed behind. After several days, they found him in the Temple sitting among the teachers. "When his parents saw him they were astonished; and his mother said to him, 'Child, why have you treated us like this? Look, your father and I have been searching for you in great anxiety.' He said to them, 'Why were you searching for me? Did you not know that I must be in my Father's house?'" (Luke 2:48-49).

In conflicts between his family identity and his mission, Jesus made his choice clear. "While he was still speaking to the crowds, his mother and his brothers were standing outside, wanting to speak to him. Someone told him, 'Look, your mother and your brothers are standing outside, wanting to speak to you.' But to the one who had told him this, Jesus replied, 'Who is my mother, and who are my brothers?' And pointing to his disciples, he said, 'Here are my mother and my brothers! For whoever does the will of my Father in heaven is my brother and sister and mother'"(Matthew 12:46-50).

Close

Join in singing the hymn used earlier in the session. Pray for families, those who help provide a positive identity for family members and those who provide a negative identity. Ask for God's grace in seeking ways to celebrate and nurture our identities as children of God.

[1] From *The Unofficial Guide to Adopting a Child*, by Andrea DellaVecchio (IDG Books Worldwide, Inc., 2000); pages 225-6.

BROKENNESS IN THE FAMILY

This session examines the sense of brokenness that often comes from difficulties within the family.

BROKEN HOME

Jan: Ryan, I know you hate the term *broken home*, but at times I feel like my family is broken. After Dad died, Mom was so consumed with grief and with working to take care of us, that she was broken. It seems like all she did was work. For a while, she worked at night as a nurse; and then during the day she would clean peoples' houses. She provided for us and made sure all three of us went to college; but in the process, her life got out of balance. I'm sure that's part of the reason she died last year. And I'm also sure that's part of the reason my brother is a workaholic.

Getting Started

Greet one another and welcome any newcomers. Take turns and describe the worst family meal you remember, either as a child or as an adult. What made that meal memorably bad? Pray for insight as the group explores the pain that is often part of family life.

Trevor: I hate the term *broken home*, too. It seems like such a cop-out. Sure, my Dad is an alcoholic. Yes, my Mom has a habit of marrying guys with problems and then trying to fix them. But all this talk about brokenness in the family seems like people trying to duck taking responsibility for their

Broken Home
During the conversation with his friends, Bill mentioned that he is scared to imagine what his son will say about him in twenty-five years. He realizes that he is not a perfect husband or a perfect father. Maria assured him that no family is perfect. She said, "I think the key is trying to figure out how to love and respect each other no matter what."

Imagine that you are talking with Bill and Maria. What would you say to them? Form groups of three or four, and discuss your response.

Talk Show
Form three groups. Each group will focus on a different person who will appear on a talk show:

- Ryan, one of the five friends we have gotten to know in this resource. Ryan has never married; in fact, he admits to being gun-shy about commitment. He felt he "was broken by the brokenness" of his family.
- Trevor, another one of the five friends, is also not sure about commitment. He lives with his girlfriend, Sandy, and has no intention of getting married. He believes that adults who blame their families for their current problems are trying to duck responsibility.
- The host of a struggling talk show. If the show is going to survive, it needs more viewers. The producers have encouraged the host to be more sensational.

After each group has a few minutes to flesh out the character of their assigned person, select one spokesperson to role-play a segment of the talk show.

own lives. If my life is messed up, it's not because my current stepfather, whom I call Dad #3, likes to spend every last dime at the race track.

Ryan: I think you guys misunderstood me. While I hated people talking about me as "poor Ryan from a broken home," it did feel like my home was broken. My life was shattered by Dad's affairs. When Mom threw him out for good, my life changed forever. My life seemed so perfect before, and afterward it was anything but perfect. I'll admit that at times I used folks' sympathy to my own advantage, but I was broken by the brokenness in my family.

Bill: One of the things that scares me about being a father is imagining what my son will say twenty-five years from now about me. As much as I love Chandra, I know I'm not the perfect husband; and even though Bill, Jr. is just a baby, already I know I'm not the perfect father. Just imagine how much I'm going to foul things up when he gets to be a teenager!

Maria: Bill, I don't think any family is perfect. We hear about "dysfunctional families" all the time, but aren't all families dysfunctional in some way? Yet there's a huge difference between families that are featured on daytime talk shows and relatively healthy families. I think the key is trying to figure out how to love and respect each other no matter what.

BROKENNESS

Jan and Ryan talk about feeling broken by family difficulties. For Jan's family, brokenness came in the death of her father and her mother's deep grief. For Ryan, his seemingly perfect life was shattered by his father's affairs and his parents' subsequent divorce. While Jan's family and Ryan's family appeared broken to those outside the family, not all broken families seem broken to others. Brokenness can take the form of divorce, violence, emotional abuse, drugs, neglect, isolation, co-dependency, compulsive gambling, workaholism, compulsive eating or dieting, sexual abuse, and more.

"Everyone has had a conflict with their family at some time or another, but for some it is more of a lifetime struggle involving much confusion and emotional pain," according to the Counseling Center at Southwest Texas State University.[1]

The term *dysfunctional family* has almost become a cliché in our society. As Maria said, "We hear about 'dysfunctional families' all the time, but aren't all families dysfunctional in some way?" Yet what is the difference between a relatively functional, healthy family and a dysfunctional, broken one?

"Family dysfunction can be any condition that interferes with healthy family functioning," states the University Counseling Service at Kansas State University. "Most families have some periods of time where functioning is impaired by stressful circumstances (death in the family, a parent's serious illness, for example). Healthy families tend to return to normal functioning after the crisis passes. In dysfunctional families, however, problems tend to be chronic and children do not consistently get their needs

SMALL GROUP

Brokenness
One definition of *family dysfunction* in this session is "any condition that interferes with healthy family functioning." What is healthy family functioning? With a partner, brainstorm characteristics of healthy family functioning. What are the things that healthy families do? After a few minutes, join another group of two to form a group of four. Discuss the characteristics of healthy family functioning you generated.

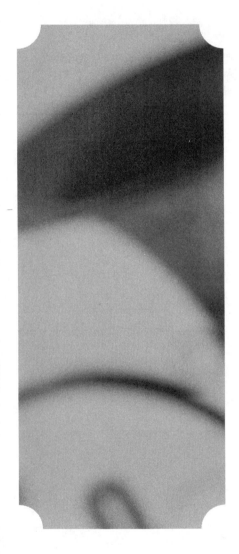

met. Negative patterns of parental behavior tend to be dominant in their children's lives."[2]

The Counseling Center at Southwest Texas State University reports that a dysfunctional family is characterized by:

- extreme rigidity in family rules;
- little or no communication;
- high levels of tension and/or arguing;
- extended periods of silence;
- blame and avoidance as primary coping mechanisms;
- overall message of "don't feel, don't talk, don't trust."[3]

The effects of growing up in a dysfunctional family often linger into adulthood. Persons raised in dysfunctional families can have difficulties maintaining healthy self-esteem, trusting others, and forming and maintaining intimate relationships. They can fear a loss of control. They often deny their own feelings. They may even deny reality.[4]

BROKEN FAMILIES IN THE BIBLE

While the term *dysfunctional family* is not found in the Bible, Scripture does include the accounts of more than a few broken families. Eli, the priest who raised Samuel, had a troubled relationship with his sons. "Now the sons of Eli were scoundrels; they had no regard for the LORD or for the duties of the priests to the people. . . . Thus the sin of the young men was very great in the sight of the LORD; for they treated the offerings of the LORD with contempt" (1 Samuel 2:12-13a, 17). Eli tried to correct his sons, but he was ineffective. "Now Eli was very old. He heard all that his sons were doing to all Israel, and how they lay with the women who served at the entrance to the tent of meeting. He said to them, 'Why do you do such things? For I hear of your evil dealings from all these people.' . . . But they would not listen to the voice of their father" (1 Samuel 2:22-23, 25c).

David had brokenness in his family. David's adultery with Bathsheba (2 Samuel 11:2-27) caused trouble. The prophet Nathan confronted the king. Speaking for God, Nathan told David, "Now therefore the sword shall never depart from your house, for you have despised me, and have taken the wife of Uriah the Hittite to be your wife. Thus says the LORD: I will raise up trouble against you from within your own house" (2 Samuel 12:10-11a). Trouble did rise in David's family. One of David's sons, Amnon, raped his half-sister Tamar. Two years later, Tamar's full-brother Absalom avenged the rape by killing Amnon (2 Samuel 13:1-29).

The trouble continued as Absalom started a civil war to gain his father's throne. While Absalom was finally defeated and killed, news of his death sent David into deep mourning. "O my son Absalom, my son, my son Absalom! Would I had died instead of you, O Absalom, my son, my son!" (2 Samuel 18:33b).

OVERCOMING BROKENNESS

It is possible to overcome the effects of being raised in a dysfunctional family. In fact, many of the survival skills people learn from being part of a dysfunctional family can be valuable in overcoming the brokenness. "People who grow up in dysfunctional families often have finely tuned empathy for others; they are often very achievement-oriented and highly successful in some areas of their lives; they are often resilient to stress and adaptive to change," according to University Counseling Services at Kansas State.[5] While some of these survival skills can be helpful, others can cause problems in adulthood.

University Counseling Services recommends the following steps to overcome brokenness:

Bible 101

One danger of studying the Bible is to read just a small portion of Scripture out of context. This can lead to a distorted understanding of Scripture. Take for example Ephesians 5:22-24: "Wives, be subject to your husbands as you are to the Lord. For the husband is the head of the wife just as Christ is the head of the church, the body of which he is the Savior. Just as the church is subject to Christ, so also wives ought to be, in everything, to their husbands." The three verses, taken alone, seem to indicate that wives are to be subservient to their husbands; after all, wives are to treat their husbands as we in the church treat Jesus Christ. This text has been used, or rather misused, to justify patriarchy, including the emotional, physical, and sexual abuse of women. However, that view is a misreading of Scripture.

The writer of Ephesians offers advice for husbands as well. "Husbands, love your wives, just as Christ loved the church and gave himself up for her. . . . In the same way, husbands should love their wives as they do their own bodies. He who loves his wife loves himself. For no one ever hates his own body, but he nourishes and tenderly cares for it, just as Christ does for the church, because we are members of his body" (Ephesians 5:25, 28-30). This text is demanding on husbands! For husbands to love their wives as Jesus Christ loves the church is no small undertaking. After all, Jesus gave up his own life for us.

Taken in context, the Ephesians passage is not directing husbands to rule over their wives however they desire. Instead, we are urged to lives of mutual love and respect. "Be subject to one another out of reverence for Christ" (Ephesians 5:21). This idea of mutual submission is valuable not only for biological families, but also for friends and for the church family. Our relationships would be transformed if we practiced mutual submission.

- Get help. This can be individual counseling or groups such as Adult Children of Alcoholics, Alanon, or Adult Children of Dysfunctional Families.
- Learn to identify and express emotions.
- Allow yourself to feel angry about what happened.
- Begin the work of learning to trust others.

Family: Finding Who We Are and How We Belong

- Practice taking good care of yourself.
- Begin to change your relationship with your family, remembering that you cannot change others; but you can change yourself.

The healing process can be long, and at times, frustrating. Many Christians draw strength from their faith when doing the healing work seems difficult or overwhelming. Remembering God's desire that we be whole, depending on God for strength, and looking to God's people—the church—for comfort, can make a difference in the healing process.

Forgiveness in the Family
Forgiveness is an important theme of the Christian faith. As such, forgiveness is also the focus of many hymns. Choose a hymn such as "Help Us Accept Each Other," "Dear Lord and Father of Mankind," or another hymn with the theme of forgiveness and sing it as a group. Discuss whether singing this hymn would be helpful for a person who has experienced family brokenness.

As an individual, or as a group, commit to serve people who may feel broken by the brokenness in their families. Ask for volunteers to find more information about possible ways to be in service. One possibility is volunteering to staff the telephone lines for a local crisis hotline. Bring the details about the service opportunity to the next session.

Close
In silence, think about any broken relationships in your life—with relatives, friends, neighbors, church members, colleagues. Confess your part in that brokenness. Pray that God will forgive you and help you find reconciliation.

[1] From "Breaking Free of Dysfunctional Family Patterns" (The Counseling Center at Southwest Texas State University, 2003); http://www.counseling.swt.edu/dysfunctional_family.htm
[2] From "Dysfunctional Families: Recognizing and Overcoming Their Effects" (University Counseling Services, Kansas State University, 1997); http://www.k-state.edu/counseling/dysfunc.html
[3] From "Breaking Free of Dysfunctional Family Patterns."
[4] From "Dysfunctional Families: Recognizing and Overcoming Their Effects."
[5] From "Dysfunctional Families: Recognizing and Overcoming Their Effects."

CHARACTERISTICS OF HEALTHY FAMILIES

This session examines the characteristics that contribute to the health
of families.

WHAT IS A HEALTHY FAMILY?

Ryan: Maria, you've said over and over again that family is important to you. I don't exactly have the best experience with family myself. I feel like I'm clueless about how to be part of a family. I know that real families aren't like the families in sit-coms. No family is perfect. So, what does a healthy family look like?

Maria: I'm certainly not an expert, and my family cer-tainly wasn't perfect; but my parents did model some things that I think are critical. Their faith was a vital part of their lives and of our family's life. We prayed together before every meal. When I was a little girl, Mom or Dad always prayed with me before I went to sleep. And church on Sunday was one of the highlights of our family's week.

Getting Started
Greet one another and welcome any newcomers. Take turns nam-ing a family you admired when you were a child. What was it that you admired about them? When everyone has named a family, reflect on your responses. Are there any common characteristics about the families the members of your group admired? Pray together: "Lord, we thank you for these families we admired as children. Help us learn what makes for healthy families, so our families can be more healthy. Amen."

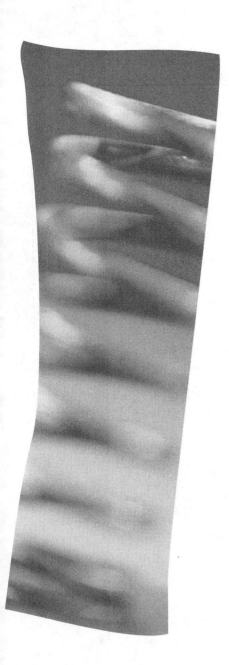

My parents always put family first, above themselves. My Dad is always saying, "There is no *I* in team, and this family is a team."

Jan: I don't know, Maria. My mom put family first, too, often without regard for her own needs. I sometimes wonder if that's why she died so young. She was so busy doing for others that she didn't take care of herself. While I agree that selfishness destroys a family, we can be destroyed as individuals if we don't take care of ourselves at all.

Trevor: Jan, you talked before about how you see the five of us as a family. I guess I do, too. I think the way we get along is great. Sure, we don't always agree with each other; but I know that each of you really cares for me. When I'm a jerk, you're willing to forgive me. We don't hold grudges. And we respect each other, even when we don't agree with each other.

Ryan: My stepfather always harps on the Bible. He says, "The Good Book says, 'Wives, be subject to your husbands as you are to the Lord. For the husband is the head of the wife just as Christ is the head of the church.'" He uses that to lord it over my mother. He treats her like dirt. I find it hard to believe that's the way God wants us to live.

Bill: It's not the way God wants us to live! Tell your stepfather to keep reading! God wants us to love each other, to respect each other, to be subject to each other. Now I understand why you think church is a waste of time! I have found that being part of a church has helped me be a better husband; and I hope it will help me be a better father, too. As I understand it, it's my job as a husband to love Chandra as much as

Christ loves the church. When you think about how much Christ loves us, that's a tremendous undertaking. The men's group at my church has been focusing on how we can learn to be that loving.

NOT PERFECT

Because of his experience growing up in a dysfunctional family, Ryan feels clueless about how to be part of a healthy family. While he recognizes that no family is perfect, what do healthy families look like?

Ryan is right; a healthy family is not the same as a perfect family. Even healthy families have misunderstanding, tension, anger, hurt, maybe even bickering and yelling from time to time. In healthy families, rules are consistent but flexible to adapt to changing circumstances; whereas in dysfunctional families, rules tend to either be inconsistent or rigid. Healthy families allow for individuality, and each individual is encouraged in his or her own interests. Family members are allowed to express their thoughts and feelings in healthy families, whereas honesty is often discouraged in dysfunctional families. In healthy families, each member is treated with respect; no one fears abuse of any kind. Healthy families recognize that everyone makes mistakes.[1]

In the Bible 101 in Session 4, we explored the danger of reading a portion of Scripture out of context and used an often misunderstood passage from Ephesians as an example. Too often, the text "Wives, be subject to your husbands as you are to the Lord" (Ephesians 5:22) has been

What Is a Healthy Family?
In the friends' discussion, Maria repeated her father's motto, "There is no *I* in team, and this family is a team." Jan said that she believes one reason her mother died so young was because that was her motto as well. She always put family first and did not take care of herself. In what ways are Maria and her father right? In what ways is Jan right? How can families learn to avoid the two extremes of selfishness that can destroy a family and individual family members being destroyed by not taking care of themselves?

Not Perfect
What does a healthy family look like? Form small groups, with each group pretending to be a creative team developing a new family situation comedy for a television network. Unlike many television series, this new show will focus on a healthy family. Each group should create a cast of characters, including important traits of each character. Be sure that each group can identify what makes this new television family different from most television families.

In small groups of three or four, discuss your responses to these questions: What characteristics of healthy families do you see in your relationships with your friends, relatives, and fellow church members? What characteristics are weak? What can you do to improve these relationships? How do the practices of faith like Bible-reading, prayer, or worship contribute to the health of family groups?

Form groups of three or four persons. Take turns and describe the best family meal you remember, either as a child or as an adult. What made that meal memorably good? After discussing your responses, bring the whole group together.

Decide how you would plan a wonderful family meal. What would be on the menu? If your group meets in the morning, plan a breakfast or brunch. If you meet in the evening, plan a dinner. Decide what each group member will bring for your family meal your next session. Each group member should bring enough copies of the recipe so every member of the group can have one.

taken out of its setting and misused to perpetrate abuse. In context, the Ephesians passage is not directing husbands to rule over their wives however they desire. Rather both husbands and wives are to value mutual love and respect. "Be subject to one another out of reverence for Christ" (Ephesians 5:21).

The writer of Ephesians also has advice for parents and children. "Children, obey your parents in the Lord, for this is right. 'Honor your father and mother'—this is the first commandment with a promise: 'so that it may be well with you and you may live long on the earth.' And, fathers, do not provoke your children to anger, but bring them up in the discipline and instruction of the Lord" (Ephesians 6:1-4). Mutual submission is valuable not only for biological families, but also for friends and for the church family.

Bible 101

The image of family is often used to describe the church, which will be explored in greater depth in Session 7. The Book of Acts describes the church in the earliest days of its existence.

In the brief description of the first days of the church (Acts 2:42-47), there are several characteristics of a healthy church family:

- The first Christians had a common devotion. They were devoted to the apostles' teaching and to growing in faith by learning from their leaders. They were devoted to fellowship and to spending time together. They were devoted to breaking bread, which in that context meant both eating together and worshiping together. They were devoted to prayer.
- They gave of what they had to those in need. Scripture does not say how long they "had all things in common," but the passage shows that generosity has been and continues to be a hallmark of genuine Christian community. Healthy church families realize that all that they have, and all that they are, comes from God and is meant for the common good.
- They had fun together. Yes, the church has a serious mission: to make disciples of Jesus Christ. However, the Christian life is a life of joy. The early Christians were known for their "glad and generous hearts."
- They were not a closed group. They reached out and included others: "Day by day the Lord added to their number those who were being saved" (verse 47).

The second edition of *From Culture Wars to Common Ground: Religion and the American Family Debate* echoes the advice from Ephesians. The authors emphasize the need for mutual love and respect, not simply the submission of wives to husbands. Mutual love and respect is valuable, not only in the relationship between husband and wife, but also between parent and child, even though children, especially young children, are dependent on their parents. While the authors recognize that a stress on love as self-sacrifice has often led to the subjugation of women within the family, they do affirm the role of self-sacrifice within the ethic of mutual love and respect.[2]

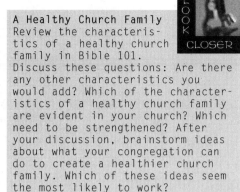

A Healthy Church Family
Review the characteristics of a healthy church family in Bible 101. Discuss these questions: Are there any other characteristics you would add? Which of the characteristics of a healthy church family are evident in your church? Which need to be strengthened? After your discussion, brainstorm ideas about what your congregation can do to create a healthier church family. Which of these ideas seem the most likely to work?

A BIBLICAL EXAMPLE

The news must have crushed Joseph. Mary, his fiancée, was pregnant; and Joseph knew he was not the father.

What would Joseph do? Breaking an engagement was not as simple at that time as it is today. Joseph and Mary were betrothed, a legally binding agreement that could only be broken by divorce. If Joseph divorced Mary and made the reason public, Mary would be disgraced. He decided to divorce Mary quietly and thus protect his own reputation and possibly shield Mary from shame. The Gospel of Matthew records, "But just when he had resolved to do this, an angel of the Lord appeared to him in a dream and said, 'Joseph, son of David, do not be afraid to take Mary as your wife, for the child conceived in her is from the Holy Spirit. She will bear a son and you are to name him Jesus, for he will save his people from their

Joseph's Dilemma
Read Matthew 1:18-19. Imagine that you are Joseph's best friend. Joseph comes to see you. He just discovered that Mary, his fiancée, is pregnant. He respects you greatly and begs for your advice. You tell Joseph that you need time to think and pray about his situation, and you promise to write him a letter. What would you write to Joseph? When you are finished writing the letter, find a partner. Read your letters to each other.

Joseph Dearest
Find copies of the traditional German Christmas carol "Joseph Dearest, Joseph Mine," and sing it together. Look closer at the first stanza. It is written from the perspective of Mary. List the ways in which Joseph's example of giving of himself for God and for his family had a positive impact on his family.

I Honor You
Do you see any clue in the vow itself how it is possible to honor your spouse, your child, your parent, your friend, or fellow church members with all that you are and all that you have? How would your relationships be affected if you honored one another this way?

In Session 4, you may have committed to serve individuals who may feel broken by the brokenness in their families. Hear reports from those who researched possible ways to be in service. Decide to which service opportunity you will commit, if possible, as a group. Establish a time to serve, and plan time to reflect on your service during the next session.

sins'" (Matthew 1:20-21). When Joseph woke up, he did as the angel commanded. Instead of focusing on saving his own reputation by divorcing Mary, he married Mary and treated Mary's son Jesus as his own son. Joseph gave of himself for God and for his family.

I HONOR YOU

As a pastor, the most significant time of the wedding for me is the exchange of rings. The new couple says to each other, "I give you this ring as a sign of my vow, and with all that I am, and all that I have, I honor you; in the name of the Father, and of the Son, and of the Holy Spirit."[3]

To honor another is not only a key to a healthy marriage. It is also a key to healthy biological families, healthy friendships, and healthy church families. When we honor another, we realize that person— be it our spouse, our child, our parent, our friend, or our fellow church member—is irreplaceable. A healthy relationship is one of mutual love and respect, when we vow to give the best of ourselves, instead of trying to get the best for ourselves.

To honor someone is to respect that person with a mixture of love and awe. To honor someone is to treat that person with dignity. And to honor someone with all that we are and all that we have is not to hold anything back. To make that vow is to promise that instead of trying to get the best for ourselves, we promise to give the best of ourselves.

Honoring another person with all that we are and all that we have is not easy, but God gives us the power to love one another that much. As we grow in our relationship with

God through worship, Bible study, prayer, and other spiritual disciplines, we discover how we can truly honor the ones we love.

Close

Sing together "Joseph Dearest, Joseph Mine." Read together the second stanza, written from Joseph's perspective. Pray together for all families, that they may be healthy, nurturing families.

[1] From "Dysfunctional Families: Recognizing and Overcoming Their Effects" (University Counseling Services, Kansas State University, 1993); *http://www.k-state.edu/counseling/dysfunc.html*

[2] From a review by Garrett Paul of *From Culture Wars to Common Ground: Religion and the American Family Debate* in *Christian Century*, May 9, 2001.

[3] From *The United Methodist Book of Worship* (The United Methodist Publishing House, 1992); pages 121-2.

CREATING HEALTHY FAMILIES

This session explores ways to build healthy families and what role Christian faith and practice can play in creating healthy families.

FOOL'S GUIDE

Ryan: I know we've talked about what a healthy family looks like, but how do we get there? Are some of us just lucky enough to be born into a good family, and the rest of us are out of luck? Or is there something we can do to create a healthy family?

Jan: My little sister is getting married next month; and as you know, I haven't exactly been thrilled with it. But she's going to get married no matter what I think. Why don't we pretend she's here with us, and we'll give her the "Fool's Guide to Creating a Healthy Family."

Bill: When Chandra and I got married, our pastor stressed the importance of honoring one another. In fact, as part of our vows, we promised to honor each other. I can remember as plain as

Getting Started
Greet one another and welcome any newcomers. Take turns and talk about your favorite family vacation, either as a child or as an adult. What made that vacation memorable? Pray that this session will help you and others in your group discover how to create a healthy family.

If the members of your group prepared a family meal as described in Session 5, eat together. Begin by singing the hymn "Be Present at Our Table, Lord," or pray a blessing. Be sure to distribute copies of each dish; and as you do, each participant should say why she or he chose that dish to prepare. Does it have any particular family memories? If so, tell about those memories.

day that when we exchanged rings I said, "Chandra, I give you this ring as a sign of my vow, and with all that I am, and all that I have, I honor you." Then Chandra said the same things to me. I truly do cherish her. And I cherish Bill Jr., too. Every day, we make sure that the three of us take time to pray together. I know Bill Jr. is too young to realize what's going on; but I want him to grow up understanding that not only do his mother and I love him, God loves him, too.

Maria: I think it's important to spend time together. When I was a child, some of the most important time we spent together as a family was going to church together. All the way home, my parents would ask us what we learned in Sunday school or how we experienced God's presence in worship. I learned that church was a great family time together. I've heard some of my coworkers try to justify how little time they spend with their children with the hackneyed line, "I might not spend much time with my children, but the time I do spend with them is quality time." Well, to a child, any time you spend with them is quality time. It's the same with adults. You can't really have a relationship with someone—be it your spouse, your children, your friends—if you don't spend time together. And when you combine making time for each other with Bill's suggestion of honoring each other, you've got it made.

Jan: I guess I would remind my sister of the importance of having fun together. That's one thing I've always loved about your family, Maria. You guys always seem to be laughing together. Our family was always so serious after Dad died. I can only remember a few times Mom ever laughing, and my brother seems to be following the same pattern. He's so serious all the time. Too serious, if you ask me.

Trevor: I would tell your sister not to forget her friends. Some married couples turn their backs on their single friends. They either spend all their time together, or they only spend time with other married couples. That's one of the things I really appreciate about you, Bill. You didn't abandon us after you got married or after Bill Jr. was born. While it's obvious that your family is important, you still make room in your life for other important relationships. Thanks.

Ryan: I would tell your sister that she should make sure that she and Greg are right for each other. She should take premarital counseling seriously. I often think that if my Mom had just known what a jerk her husband is before they got married, she never would have married him.

Fool's Guide
Review the discussion of the five friends. Each of the five had suggestions for how to create a healthy family. Of the advice given, which one do you think is best? Why? If you were the sixth person in that discussion, what suggestion of how to create a healthy family would you add? How can Christian faith help in creating a healthy family?

RIGHT FOR EACH OTHER

Ryan suggested that Jan's sister and her fiancée make sure they are right for each other, and he encouraged them to take premarital counseling seriously. While counseling cannot guarantee marital success, it can help couples enter marriage with their eyes open.

"The majority of divorce-causing issues already exists before the wedding," according to Corey Donaldson, who interviewed six hundred divorced people before writing *Don't You Dare Get Married Until You Read This!* Donaldson said that asking challenging questions before the wedding can prevent heartaches after the wedding.[1]

One of the most insightful questions is: Would you ever consider trading in your

Right for Each Other
Form teams of three or four people. Imagine that you work for a psychological assessment company. Your team has been selected to develop a questionnaire for couples considering marriage. Your first task is to brainstorm possible questions to include. Have the small groups report on their questions to the whole group.

engagement ring for a bigger and better diamond? Diamond Cutters International asked 200 new brides that question in 1988; 46 percent said yes, and 54 percent said no. The same women were polled again 15 years later. Among those who said no, they would not trade for a bigger and better diamond, 78 percent remain married. Of those who said yes, they would trade up, 81 percent are now divorced. "The results suggest people 'hard-wired' to upgrade rings also may be driven to upgrade cars, houses and eventually spouses," said psychiatrist Francisco Montalvo.[2]

INGREDIENTS FOR A HEALTHY FAMILY

Don Dinkmeyer and Gary D. McKay suggest four basic ingredients for building positive relationships in their resource *The Parent's Handbook: Systematic Training for Effective Parenting.* While Dinkmeyer and McKay focus their work on the relationship of parent and child, following these suggestions will strengthen any relationship, including among spouses, friends, and church members.

1. Mutual respect. "Nagging, yelling, hitting, talking down, doing things for children that they can do for themselves, following double standards— all show lack of respect," write Dinkmeyer and McKay. "To establish mutual respect, we must be willing to begin by demonstrating respect."
2. Taking time for fun. "In the busy pace of modern life, it's often easy to overlook this important aspect for building a positive family relationship," according to Dinkmeyer and McKay. They

recommend that families with children spend time having fun together at least once a week. Taking time for fun is also important to build a strong relationship among friends, church members, and couples without children.

3. Encouragement. "We must believe in our children if they are to believe in themselves," write Dinkmeyer and McKay. "To feel adequate, children need frequent encouragement." Adults need frequent encouragement as well. Encouragement involves recognizing another person's assets and strengths while minimizing the importance of mistakes.

4. Communicating love. How often do we tell members of our families and our friends we love them, both by what we say and by what we do? Unexpected loving comments, notes and non-verbal signs such as pats and hugs can be especially important.[3]

Ingredients for a Healthy Family
Review Don Dinkmeyer and Gary D. McKay's four basic ingredients for building positive relationships in their resource *Systematic Training for Effective Parenting.* How would these ingredients help create healthier relationships with relatives? with friends? with church members? What ingredients would you add? What role do you think the practices of Christian faith play in assessing ways to create a healthy family?

REACHING OUT

In Bible 101 during Session 6, we noted that one characteristic of the early church was that it was not a closed group. The church reached out and included others. That quality is also important in helping to create healthy families. For biological families, this can mean being sure to spend time with friends, including those who have children and those who do not have children, those who are married and those who are single.

This would be a relief to the life of the title character in Helen Fielding's novel *Bridget Jones's Diary.* At one social func-

Reaching Out
Imagine that you are a friend and neighbor of Bridget Jones and a member of a nearby church. Bridget informs you of the above conversations, and you decide to approach some leaders of your church so they can discuss how to be more open to all people, including "singletons." How might single persons identify and create healthy family structures in their lives? How would you suggest the church recognize and address the needs of single persons? What ministries might address the needs of single persons?

Sing together the hymn "Happy the Home When God Is There." After you sing, focus your attention on the stanza "Lord, let us in our homes agree this blessed peace to gain; / unite our hearts in love to thee, and love to all will reign."

Designate three areas of your meeting space: One is "The Answer," another "Part of the Answer," and the third "Not the Answer." Ask members of the group to move to the area that most closely describes their response to this question: Will uniting the hearts of family members in love to God help love reign in the family? Have the members of each group list the reasons for their response. Bring the whole group together to hear reports from the smaller groups. Then discuss in what ways uniting the hearts of family members in love to God will help love to reign in the family.

Imagine a friend of yours is about to get married. Your friend knows you have been studying this resource and wants your insight on what to do to create a healthy family. While you plead that you are by no means an expert on family, your friend insists. You agree to do so. Write a letter to your friend with your opinion on the keys to creating a healthy family.

tion, Geoffrey says to Bridget, "So you still haven't got a feller?"

"Bridget! What are we going to do with you!" said Una. "You career girls! I don't know! Can't put it off forever, you know. Tick-tock-tick-tock."

"Yes. How does a woman manage to get to your age without being married," roared Brian Enderby.[4]

Later in the book, after another uncomfortable encounter with married couples, Bridget calls a friend, who suggests, "You should have said, 'I'm not married because I'm a *Singleton*, you smug, prematurely aging, narrow-minded morons.'"[5]

FAMILY-FRIENDLY?

The authors of *From Culture Wars to Common Ground: Religion and the American Family* recommend some steps to make our society more family friendly. Suggestions include having government-supported marriage and family education, making divorce laws more child-friendly, and developing more family-friendly workplaces. The authors also suggest that churches should address the needs of both two-parent families and other types of families.[6]

If churches are "to thrive and remain true to their deepest theological commitments, they must reach out to America's growing ranks of unconventional families. They must develop programs for divorced men and women, single parents and cohabiting couples," writes W. Bradford Wilcox. "On the other hand . . . churches must do more to articulate a substantive vision of family that confronts the mounting evidence that divorce and out-of-wedlock childbearing pose serious threats to children."[7]

Family Friendly
Imagine that your group is a task force generating ideas of how your congregation can truly be family friendly. Brainstorm your ideas, being sure to consider the need to reach out to unconventional families and the need to have a vision of family that takes seriously the evidence of the threats to children. Make a list of your ideas. Choose one that seems appropriate for the needs of your community and take the steps to make this idea a working ministry in your congregation.

First Corinthians 13, often called the "Love Chapter," is one of the most common Bible texts read at weddings. However, Paul did not write these words to people who were about to get married. Instead, it is intended for all Christians and is sound advice for people in any relationship, including the relationship of husband and wife. Paul suggests that we build all our relationships—marriage, friendships, congregations—on the solid base of the love God shares with us in Jesus Christ.

Read 1 Corinthians 13:1-8a. Paul wrote these as part of his response to problems reported to him by some of the Christians in Corinth. Imagine that you are in Corinth and wrote one of the letters to Paul that caused Paul to write his letter. What did you say in your letter? When you are finished, exchange letters with a partner.

Paul understood that God's love for us is much more than a feeling. It is that deep love that God freely gives us, that we are to share with each other in marriage and in all our other relationships. Just as God loves us patiently, so we are to love each other patiently, even when the one we love turns away from us. Just as God's love for us is kind, so we are to be kind in our love for each other. We are to offer the best to each other, even if the receiver of our love does not always deserve the best by his or her actions. And just as God's love for us does not insist on its own way, so we are not to insist on our own way in our love. We are to love others by being a servant instead of being self-serving.

Close
Close with prayer. Pray that God may grant all participants in your group guidance and strength as you create a healthy family.

Loving others as God loves us is a lot of work. Who of us can love like that? Who of us can be that patient, that kind, that considerate? The truth is none of us can do it if we rely only on ourselves; but if we allow God to be an active partner in our marriages, our friendships, and our congregations, we can build strong, healthy family relationships.

[1] Reported in *The Wilmington Delaware News Journal,* March 11, 2003.
[2] From *The Wilmington Delaware News Journal.*
[3] From *The Parent's Handbook: Systematic Training for Effective Parenting,* by Don Dinkmeyer and Gary D. McKay (American Guidance Service, Inc., 1989); pages 12-13.
[4] From *Bridget Jones's Diary,* by Helen Fielding (Viking, 1996); page 11.
[5] From *Bridget Jones's Diary;* page 37.
[6] From a review by Garrett Paul of *From Culture Wars to Common Ground: Religion and the American Family Debate* in *Christian Century,* May 9, 2001.
[7] From "Churches' Witness on the Family Mixed Messages," by W. Bradford Wilcox in *Christian Century,* February 21, 2001.

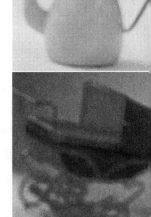

Session 7

GOD'S FAMILY

In this session we discover how the church is a family of faith.

Looking for a Home

Trevor: Sandy and I have been talking about maybe going to church, but we really don't know what to look for in a church. She's never been part of a church, and my experiences with church haven't always been pleasant. Folks at times seem so judgmental; and since Sandy and I are living together, I'm kind of afraid of what reaction we'll get from church people once they figure out we're "living in sin."

Maria: For me, it's really important that a church be a warm, welcoming place. Back in my freshman year of college I was looking for a church. This one church seemed to have everything: a great choir, a beautiful building, an inspiring preacher; but no one said a word to me the first time I went. Or the second time. Or the third time. I felt like they couldn't care less if I was there or not. So I started going to another church a little farther away from my dorm. While the choir

Getting Started
Greet one another and welcome any newcomers. Imagine that a friend of yours was looking for a church. What are the positives about your church that you would be sure to tell them? Pray together. Begin by offering thanks to God for your church and for its positive attributes.

Looking for a Home
Trevor told his friends that he and Sandy have been talking about going to church. Brainstorm a list of characteristics you would suggest important to help Trevor and Sandy in their search. After the group has generated ideas, decide which characteristics are most important. Why do you think the characteristics you chose are important?

Family Friendly
Imagine that your group is a task force generating ideas of how your congregation can truly be family friendly. Brainstorm your ideas, being sure to consider the need to reach out to unconventional families and the need to have a vision of family that takes seriously the evidence of the threats to children. Make a list of your ideas. Choose one that seems appropriate for the needs of your community and take the steps to make this idea a working ministry in your congregation.

wasn't as good, and the building was a little run down, the people really cared for each other and for me. I was treated like a sister in Christ and felt like I was welcomed into a family.

Ryan: I got turned off from church by my stepfather. He's always quoting "the Good Book" to justify his behavior. He's such a hypocrite. He treats Mom like dirt, he's always been a jerk to me, and yet he's considered a respected leader in the church. I just don't get it. Shouldn't church people live good lives? I figure if someone like that is included in the church, then I don't want to be.

Jan: I can see your point, Ryan; but it doesn't seem fair to judge all churches because of your stepfather. I know you've had a horrible experience with the church, but don't let that stop you from experiencing the good that being part of God's family can bring. Among the things that have kept me going since Mom died are you guys and my church. Maria invited me to church right after Mom died, and she didn't take no for an answer. Thanks, Maria.

Bill: My church is really big, yet we've found a home there. We're part of a small group with other married couples, and it's a great way to get support for the challenges of marriage and having a baby. I'm also part of a men's group at church, and those two groups are like an extended family for me.

CHURCH FAMILY

Maria, Jan, and Bill have each found a church home. Maria talked about being treated like a sister in Christ and felt that she was welcomed into a family. Bill said that two small groups at his church are like an extended family.

I know what they mean. As a young child, my church was very much an extended family. In fact, some of the adults in the church I called "aunt" and "uncle." I was quite confused later to discover that Aunt Ramona, Uncle Bill, Aunt Dot, and Uncle Jim were not blood relatives at all; but they were like a family to me. Some were occasional babysitters. Others sat with me during worship while my mother sang in the choir. They took seriously their commitment to surround me with care and love so that I could grow in my trust of God and be found faithful in my service to others, as stated in the baptismal liturgy.

MUSIC

As a group, sing the hymn "Blest Be the Tie That Binds." Look more closely at the stanza "We share each other's woes, our mutual burdens bear; / and often for each other flows the sympathizing tear." How is the church described as a family in that stanza? in the rest of the hymn?

FAMILY IMAGES IN SCRIPTURE

In Bible 101 during Session 3, we looked at Matthew 12:46-50. Clearly, Jesus saw the community that was gathering around him as a family of faith.

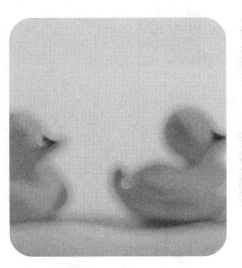

Paul, one of the early leaders of the church, also used the image of family to describe the church. In his letter to the Galatians, Paul used the family metaphor several times. He opened the letter with these words: "Paul an apostle—sent neither by human commission nor from human authorities, but through Jesus Christ and God the Father, who raised him from the dead—and all the members of God's family who are with me" (Galatians 1:1-2a). Several times, Paul referred to the Galatian Christians as "brothers and sisters" (1:11; 3:15; 5:13). He reminded them that "in Christ Jesus you are all children of God through faith" (3:26); and "if you belong to Christ, then

Letter to the Church
In this session, we look at Paul's letter to the churches in Galatia. He used family language to address the Galatians, to encourage them to care for one another and to recognize their connection with one another and with God. Imagine Paul writing a letter to your church. What would he say? Write a letter from Paul's perspective. When you finish writing, exchange letters with another participant.

Create a sculpture of your church using modeling clay or playdough (a recipe is included). This could be either a model of the church building or an abstract sculpture capturing some element of your congregation.

Playdough
1 cup flour (not self-rising)
½ cup salt
1 tablespoon cooking oil
1 teaspoon cream of tartar
1 cup water
1 teaspoon food coloring

Mix together flour, salt, and cream of tartar in a saucepan. Mix water, oil, and food coloring. Add to flour mixture, stirring constantly, over medium high heat until mixture forms a soft dough ball in pan. Cool and knead until smooth and elastic, adding more flour if needed. Store in an airtight container. Lasts for months! The recipe can be doubled easily.[1]

you are Abraham's offspring, heirs according to the promise" (3:29).

Paul admonished the Galatian Christians to care for one another as family (6:10). He also used the language of adoption: "But when the fullness of time had come, God sent his Son, born of a woman, born under the law, in order to redeem those who were under the law, so that we might receive adoption as children. And because you are children, God has sent the Spirit of his Son into our hearts, crying, 'Abba! Father!'" (4:4-6). Perhaps most surprising is language Paul used to describe his relationship with the Galatians: "My little children, for whom I am again in the pain of childbirth until Christ is formed in you" (4:19).

The church is a family of faith because:

- the members of the church are all children of God.
- the members of the church are committed to do the will of God.
- the members of the church vow to work for the common good and to care for each other as a family.

BROKENNESS IN THE CHURCH FAMILY

Just as there can be brokenness in our biological families, so there can be brokenness in a church family. This brokenness arose in the early days of the church. The Book of Acts records that Hellenists, the term used for primarily Greek-speaking Jewish-Christians, felt that their needs were being overlooked. In particular, the Hellenists believed that their widows were neglected in the daily distribution of food, while the widows of the Hebrews, the term used for primarily Hebrew- or Aramaic-speaking Jewish Christians, received enough food. This complaint, as minor as it may seem to us, had the potential to rip apart the young church. Would the church family be able to stay unified even with its cultural differences?

The Hellenists brought their complaint to the leaders of the church, the Twelve, who brought together the whole community and said that they could not neglect their current duties (what is called "the word of God") in order to serve the widows. Instead, seven followers were selected as the first deacons. Their responsibility was to serve those in need, both Hellenists and Hebrews. It is significant that the seven selected—Stephen, Philip, Prochorus, Nicanor, Timon, Parmenas, and Nicolaus—all had Greek names. Instead of being torn apart, the church continued to flourish: "The word of God continued to spread; the number of the disciples increased greatly in Jerusalem" (Acts 6:7).

Congregations today have conflicts as well, everything from budget priorities to the color of the carpet. These disagreements, which are usually minor, have the potential to rip apart church families. During tense times, it may be tempting to either try to ignore the conflict or leave the church in order to get away from it. Yet, just as the early church found a solution and thrived, so our congregations can do the same.

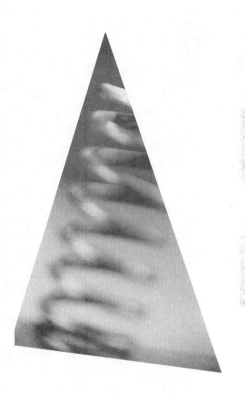

A BELOVED BROTHER

Philemon, one of the shortest books in the New Testament, witnesses to the revolutionary potential of understanding the

---

A Beloved Brother
Imagine that you are Onesimus. Your friend and mentor Paul discovers that you are a runaway slave. He sends you back to your master Philemon armed only with a letter. On your way back, you decide to write a letter of your own. What would you write your master? Form groups of three or four, and read your letters to one another.

In the discussion among the five friends, Trevor mentioned that he and Sandy are talking about going to church. Most likely, there are many people in your community who are also talking about going to church. One way to serve these persons is to print a guide to churches in your area. As a group, be sure to have volunteers:

- contact each church in the area encouraging them to be part of the project by providing brief information about the congregation.
- obtain funding to print the guide. You may want to ask participating churches to give money to offset the cost of production or ask individuals to sponsor the guide.
- produce the guide, including compiling the information from the various churches, word processing, editing, and printing.
- create and implement a distribution system for the guide.

Close
Form a circle. In silence, take a moment to look around at all the group members. Give thanks to God for each person who has participated in this study with you. Conclude in prayer, being sure to give thanks to God for this study, for the gift of family—including the church family—and for each person in the group.

church as a family of faith. Paul wrote this letter to Philemon, his "dear friend and co-worker." While imprisoned in Rome, Paul became close friends with Onesimus. In fact, Onesimus was very useful in Paul's ministry. In time, Paul discovered that Onesimus was a runaway slave belonging to Philemon.

Paul wrote: "I am sending him, that is, my own heart, back to you. I wanted to keep him with me, so that he might be of service to me in your place during my imprisonment for the gospel; but I preferred to do nothing without your consent, in order that your good deed might be voluntary and not something forced. Perhaps this is the reason he was separated from you for a while, so that you might have him back forever, no longer as a slave but more than a slave, a beloved brother—especially to me but how much more to you" (Philemon 12-16).

Paul's plea is earthshaking. Philemon had every legal right to punish Onesimus. Instead, Paul urges Philemon to welcome him back as a brother. This brief letter reinforces that if Christians are brothers and sisters in Christ, if we are all children of God, if we are all committed to do the will of God, and if we all vow to work for the common good and to care for each other like a family, then we all have equal status within the church.

[1] From *The Calvary United Methodist Church Cookbook* (Calvary United Methodist Church, Queenstown, Maryland); page 47.

CASE STUDIES

Getting Started

Use any of these cases in place of or in addition to the cases in the sessions as a means of stimulating discussion.

Grace Church

Because of your participation in this study, you have been asked to be a consultant for Grace Church's family ministries task force. While you do not feel like an expert in family ministries, you agreed to consult with the church because the task force wanted someone with an outside perspective.

The task force members are:

- Anne, 63, has been married for 37 years. She and her husband, Bob, have three children and three grandchildren. Helen is an elementary school teacher. Karen is divorced and lives with her son in another state. Bob Jr. and his wife Stacy are members of the church, but they and their two children only attend worship on Christmas Eve and Easter and are involved in no other ministries of the church.
- Stan, 35, divorced two years ago. His ex-wife, Lisa, used to be a member of the church; but after the divorce, she stopped going. Their three children, ages 5 through 9, live with Stan every weekend and with Lisa during the week. Stan works at a local bank.
- Graciela, 29, has been married for four years. She and her husband Antonio have a 9-month-old daughter. They joined the church two years ago when they moved to town. Last week Graciela went back to work as a nurse at the end of her maternity leave.
- Helen, 28, has been married to Perry for five years. She is pregnant with their first child, who is due in three months. She and Perry have not decided how long they will each take for parental leave. Helen is not sure when she wants to return to work as a social worker after the baby is born.
- Tony, 27, calls himself the token bachelor. He has never married. He grew up in the church. Tony agreed to serve on the task force when he was asked, but he wonders what his role is. Tony works in advertising for the local newspaper.
- Tina, 31, married Roger last year. This is Tina's first marriage, but Roger has two children from a previous marriage. The children, ages 7 and 10, live with them every other week. Tina is a real estate agent.

Case Studies

- Pat, 38, has been married to Lou for 15 years. They have two children, ages 6 and 10. Pat is a stay-at-home mom and is the chairperson of the task force.

The first meeting you attend is the seventh meeting of the task force. In previous meetings, the group narrowed their proposals to the following:

- Start a Divorce Recovery ministry to address the needs of those who are divorced, including support groups for men and women, and social activities. The proposal also incorporates social activities and access to counseling for children whose parents are divorced.
- Begin a Families 'R Fun ministry, which will be a fellowship group for families (both singles and couples) with children from birth through sixth grade. The group's monthly activities will be designed to give families a chance to enjoy and nurture their own families and one another.
- Offer parenting classes, although the task force has yet to decide which curriculum to use. One option is from a well-regarded Christian organization. The other is from an equally well-regarded secular counseling organization that includes a special biblical supplement. Some group members argue that the first option is too conservative, while others say the second option is too liberal.

The task force members agree that because of limited resources of finances, time, energy, and people, the church cannot choose all of the options.

What advice would you give?

Neighbors

Your friends, Clark and Terry, who are in their mid-20s, just moved into a new neighborhood four months ago after their wedding. One day when you are visiting them, they ask for your insight into a dilemma.

Their next-door neighbors are a family with three children: Tim, 7; Caroline, 4; and Michelle, 2. Tim has latched on to Terry and Clark and is often over at their house. Almost every Saturday and Sunday afternoon, Tim crosses the street and knocks on Clark and Terry's door. His parents, Barbara and Paul, are so busy with the two younger children that they do not seem to care when Tim goes across the street.

While your friends like children, they have some concerns. First, Tim spends so much time with them on the weekends, that Terry and Clark feel they have little time to themselves. Second, they have observed that Paul and Barbara often seem overwhelmed with the children and working. Third, Terry noticed that Tim is not very gentle when playing with their cat. Fourth,

Clark recently found out that a family down the street no longer allows Tim into their home because of what the neighbors termed "inappropriate play" with their five-year-old son.

What would you suggest your friends do?

Family Reunion

Your friend David asked for your opinion. He explained that his extended family has a reunion every five years, and he has been appointed to the planning committee. Since the last family reunion, his Aunt Sally, his father's youngest sister, died suddenly at age 44. Six months later, her husband, Matt, moved in with a 28-year-old woman named Georgia. Matt's children, David's youngest cousins, are 14 and 16; and they live with their father and Georgia. Some members of the family reunion committee are incensed with the arrangement. They feel that not enough time passed after Sally's death. Others feel that the arrangement is sinful since Matt and Georgia are not married and because Georgia is so much younger than Matt. They have said that they should not invite them to the reunion. Others believe that Matt and Georgia and the boys should be invited, no matter what. Matt has been part of the family for years, and certainly the boys should not be excluded. David is not sure what to do.

What would you tell David?

SERVICE LEARNING OPTIONS

Use one or more of these ideas to help enrich your learning about family.

Idea #1: Adopt a Grandparent

Ask your pastor if there is an older member of the church who does not have family living in the area. Either as an individual, with some friends, with your family, or as a study group, ask the suggested person if he or she would be interested in being adopted as a grandparent. Come up with a covenant together about how your relationship will work. Some ideas: Agree to pray for each other, have a meal together on a regular basis—either by taking turns hosting or going out to eat—sit together during worship, or exchange cards and perhaps gifts for important holidays and birthdays. If possible, get to know your newly adopted grandparent's family when they visit.

Idea #2: Kids Night Out

Many couples with young children have difficulty finding reliable, afford-able, available babysitters. Many singles and couples without children enjoy spending time with children. As a group, consider sponsoring a regular Kids Night Out for your church and/or community. This could be done once a month or a few times a year. For Kids Night Out, have a child-friendly meal, games, and other activities for the children. While charging a fee for each child will help pay for the evening and build commitment from the parents that their children will come if registered, keep the fee low.

Idea #3 Help for Broken Families

In Session 4, we focused on brokenness in the family. As an individual or a group, consider offering help for broken families. Two options are:

- Call a local shelter for abused women and children. Ask what help is most needed. It could be volunteering at the shelter (serving a meal, clerical assistance, job training, babysitting), providing for physical needs (clothing, bedding), or some other assistance. If possible, provide this help on a regular basis.
- Contact the government agency in charge of foster care in your area. Ask what help children in the foster care system most need. Some ideas could

be: gifts of school supplies in the fall, Christmas gifts, stuffed animals, duffel bags or suitcases (many children who move from one foster family to another, or who move out of the foster care system, have to use trash bags to move their clothing and other belongings), or gift certificates to child-friendly restaurants for the child and his or her foster family.

Idea #4 Holiday Celebration With the Church Family

In Session 7, we explored how the church is a family of faith. Several members of the church are not able to spend holidays such as Thanksgiving, Christmas, or Easter with their families, either because of geographic or emotional distance. As an individual or a group, organize a holiday celebration as a church family for those who are interested. Ask the pastor for the names and addresses of church members who most likely will not spend the holiday with their families. Some ideas: Have a Thanksgiving covered dish dinner at church, have a Christmas caroling party and/or gift exchange, pair up interested households (which can be singles, couples without children, or couples with children) to determine how they will celebrate the next holiday together.